GW00838624

FOREWORD

More than twenty years after the ground-breaking Warnock Report, meeting the needs of children with special educational needs (SEN) remains a rewarding but challenging area for all educators. During that time, thanks to the pioneering work of a number of LEAs and schools, a consensus on the advantages of an inclusive approach to SEN provision has now emerged, to the extent that it is now a policy adopted by Government. As a result, there was a flurry of activity on the special needs front during 2001, with a revision of the SEN Code of Practice and the passing of the SEN and Disability Act.

At the same time, specialist support for classroom teachers and their pupils, which became more widely available following the 1981 Education Act, has been increasingly eroded as the role of LEAs has diminished and an increasing proportion of funding has been delegated to schools. In many parts of the country, LEA special needs support services have been disbanded. This is at a time when the benefits of inclusion in mainstream schools for children with SEN are being more widely recognised.

I am therefore particularly pleased to endorse this timely revision of **Achievement for all**, a publication which has proved a valuable resource for teachers and support staff, and which has also been widely used in initial teacher training.

The Association of Teachers and Lecturers (ATL), and its Special Educational Needs Advisory Committee in particular, has played a key role in consultations with Government concerning the revised SEN Code of Practice, the SEN and Disability Act and the Disability Rights Commission's consultation on its new Code of Practice for schools. This ensures that the commitment to an inclusive approach to special needs goes forward in full awareness of the resource implications (in terms of professional development and access to in-class support and resources) as perceived by classroom teachers and education support staff.

My thanks go to the members of the Committee who contributed to this revision. I am sure that this publication will continue to serve its purpose as a frequently and easily used point of reference which will continue to sustain the Association of Teachers and Lecturers' reputation for high-quality support in the field of special educational needs.

Julie Grant
President of the Association of Teachers and Lecturers
2001-2002

CONTENTS

The term **special educational needs** (SEN) was first used in the Warnock Report of 1978 and then in the 1981 Education Act in an attempt to focus on the needs of each individual child rather than on categories of disability. However, it is not possible or helpful to ignore categories altogether and some are still used to describe different kinds of provision. The chapters in this publication are based on the main areas of difficulty embraced by the term **special educational needs**.

Following the 1993 Education Act, a Code of Practice regarding provision for children with special educational needs came into force in September 1994. This identified a five-stage approach to the identification and assessment of special educational needs. Although the Code of Practice raised the profile of special educational needs and established nationally agreed procedures, it soon became clear to teachers in mainstream education that the Code was a long way short of a panacea. The increasing amount of paperwork required to gain support for a child added to the bureaucratic burden, and the time taken to assess a child's needs varied widely across the country. Over the years that followed, concerns grew as cash-strapped education authorities closed support services and openly admitted that they needed to cut down on formal assessments.

In 1998 the Government's Green Paper **'Excellence for All Children'** recommended greater inclusion of children with special educational needs into mainstream education. While the Association of Teachers and Lecturers agreed in principle with the idea of inclusion, it also cautioned against the wholesale closure of special schools on the grounds that the interests of the child must remain paramount.

In the light of concerns – voiced particularly by Ofsted and the Audit Commission – about how the Code of Practice was working, a revised version was issued for implementation from 1st January 2002.

The main changes in the 2002 Code of Practice are:
- the right for children with special educational needs to be educated in a mainstream school is strengthened

- LEAs have new duties to provide advice and information for parents and a means of resolving disputes

- schools and nursery education providers have a new duty to inform parents when making special educational needs provision for their child

- schools have the right to request a statutory assessment of a child.

The revised Code of Practice replaces the five stages of provision with a 'graduated approach' under the headings **'School Action'** and **'School Action Plus'**. Assessment is not to be regarded as a single, time-consuming event but as a continuing process.

The main emphases of the Code of Practice are:
- early intervention

- the planning and strategic functions of schools and LEAs

- accountability for special educational needs funds

- support for the Special Educational Needs Co-ordinator (SENCo) by provision of non-contact time, IT support and clerical assistance

- the writing of statements.

The Code of Practice's main focus is on teaching, learning and achievement, rather than on bureaucratic procedures.

The previous seven categories of need are replaced by the following four areas of need:
- communication and interaction

- cognition and learning

- behaviour, emotional and social development

- sensory and/or physical needs.

Increased weighting is given to:
- child participation and the voice of the child

- partnership with parents

- an improved partnership between schools and other agencies (e.g. health and social services). The Code of Practice calls for 'a seamless service'.

From September 2001, infant class sizes were limited to 30 by law. However, the Code of Practice makes an exception for children from special schools attending mainstream classes.

Children with a statement naming the school can be admitted outside the normal admission round, but for that school year only.

In an attempt to reduce bureaucracy, **Individual Education Plans (IEPs)** now only record what is additional to or different from curriculum plans (that already show differentiation as part of normal provision). IEPs are to be concise, with a maximum of three to four targets.

In a welcome change, speech and language therapy are normally to be regarded as part of education, rather than health, provision.

The timescale for the production of statements is set at a maximum of 26 weeks.

From Year 9 on, **Transition Plans** are to be put in place for children leaving school.

The push for greater inclusion was given further impetus by the passing of the Special Educational Needs and Disability Act 2001. The provisions came into force in January 2002, and the disability provisions from September 2002.

The main points of the Special Educational Needs and Disability Act 2001 follow.

- The right of children with a statement to a place in a mainstream school (if parents wish) is strengthened, as long as this is not incompatible with the efficient education of other children.

- LEAs are to establish **Parent Partnerships** services.

- Statutory guidance is to be published.

There are two core duties for schools and LEAs:

- not to treat a disabled child 'less favourably' for a reason relating to his/her disability

- to make reasonable adjustments as required by the child.

The legislation applies to every aspect of school life (admissions, exclusions, curriculum, breaks and lunchtimes, discipline policies, extra-curricular activities, educational visits and school journeys, for example).

There are two exemptions:

- there is no requirement to provide auxiliary aids and services, because these are to be accessed via the SEN route

- there is no requirement to make physical alterations, because this is covered via the planning duty.

LEAs in England and Wales are under a duty to plan to:

- increase access to school buildings for disabled children

- increase access to the curriculum for disabled children

- improve the delivery of information provided in writing to children who are disabled (e.g. visually impaired).

The SEN Tribunal is re-constituted as the SEN and Disability Tribunal.

*For reasons of consistency, **Achievement for all** refers to 'the teacher'. Please note however that the advice and information contained in these pages has also been prepared for the use of non-teaching professionals who are directly involved in the delivery of education, and for lecturers. Similarly, this publication generally refers to 'the child', but the term should also be read to include older students, to whom we would generally refer to as 'young people'.*

About this publication

This publication, written by the Association of Teachers and Lecturers SEN Advisory Committee, draws on the expertise of many members who have willingly shared experience gained over many years in both mainstream and specialist settings.

We hope that the information presented in this book is as comprehensive and practical as possible. Our goal is that children with special educational needs and their peers can experience an environment where they can learn from each other and can make a valued contribution to the life of the school or college.

COGNITION AND LEARNING
Children with learning difficulties

1

Children with learning difficulties form the largest group of children with special educational needs. Learning difficulties range from mild, through moderate, to severe.

o Children with mild learning difficulties generally experience problems in acquiring basic literacy and numeracy skills.

o Children with moderate learning difficulties may also have problems with speech and language development and/or emotional or behavioural difficulties.

o Children with severe learning difficulties are likely to have major problems in some or all of these areas, and possibly difficulties with personal care.

Children with learning difficulties will find it hard to keep up in all, or most, of the academic areas of the curriculum. Their all-round development is likely to be delayed, so they may be socially and emotionally immature and may have problems with gross and fine motor skills. Unless these children receive considerable support, their difficulties will become increasingly apparent throughout their education. They are unlikely to progress as quickly as their peers, and there will be a tendency for the gap to widen with every passing year.

Children with learning difficulties are inclined to rely more heavily on adult support than their peers. As there is little incidental learning and an inability to generalise, they need carefully structured teaching where new skills are built up step by step.

Children with Down's Syndrome usually fall somewhere in the general range of slower learners. Some have additional problems, such as a hearing loss.

Identification
Children with learning difficulties are usually identified by their teachers at an early stage. It may be helpful however to bear in mind that they exhibit some of the following characteristics:

- slowness in picking up new ideas

- an inability to remember new skills without constant reinforcement and repetition – to the point of over-learning

- difficulty in absorbing abstract ideas

- a lack of imagination

- poor listening skills and difficulty in following instructions addressed to the class as a whole

- poor concentration and a short attention span

- immature speech and phraseology, coupled with a limited vocabulary (slow learners may prefer giving one-word answers)

- problems remembering what they have seen or heard

- poor co-ordination, affecting both gross and fine motor skills

- responding best to being given practical experience and apparatus to support their learning

- slowness in learning to read, and then a tendency to read 'parrot fashion' with understanding lagging behind

- slowness to establish number concepts

- tendency to gravitate towards younger children rather than socialising with their peer group.

Your thoughts

Strategies

Whereas children with severe learning difficulties may be unaware of their weaknesses, other slow learners may be all too conscious that they are progressing less well than their classmates. Everything possible must therefore be done to enhance their self-esteem. Some children may be so aware of failing that they begin to believe they are incapable of learning. They need to be convinced that, although they may not find it easy, they can and will learn if they persevere.

Some of the following strategies may help to support children with learning difficulties.

- Establish what the child knows, and go back to the point at which the difficulty starts to occur.

- Allow the child to work at his/her own pace, setting tasks that can be realistically completed within the time available.

- Structure learning in small stages and in a sequential manner – a child cannot be expected to understand place value, for example, if he or she does not have a thorough mastery of number bonds.

- Present the same concept in a variety of ways, so that learning is reinforced.

- Find time for frequent repetition of routine learning (e.g. reciting tables and the alphabet, learning to read and spelling key words).

- Remember that short, daily repetition is more valuable than longer, weekly sessions.

- Show the child what to do as well as talking about it. Give concrete examples and allow practical apparatus to be used for as long as it is needed.

- Keep tasks short, and work towards a gradual increase in concentration.

- Encourage a passive child to become more actively involved in discussion and group activities to give him or her the practice needed.

- Provide a starting point for creative writing tasks, rather than presenting the child with a blank sheet of paper.

- Teach study skills at all levels, so that the child has access to sources of help.

- Listen to what the learner is saying, so that his/her viewpoint is understood and any distress becomes apparent.

- Provide immediate feedback to reward effort.

- Publicly acknowledge the child's talents so that he or she has status within the group.

- Give the child experience of success in the non-verbal areas of the curriculum where he or she can excel.

- Discuss evidence of progress with the child.

A child may appear unmotivated because the task, or the way it is presented, is inappropriate. Try, as far as possible, to differentiate tasks and materials so that the child can be motivated through achieving success. Instructions may need to be repeated in different ways (as a check, the child can be asked to say what he or she has been asked to do), and it is best to avoid giving too much information at once. Almost every child responds to praise and encouragement, and such strategies are particularly helpful in raising the self-esteem of learners.

Specific learning difficulties

DYSLEXIA

Children with specific learning difficulties may exhibit an uneven pattern of strengths and weaknesses. There is likely to be a discrepancy between their verbal and/or practical abilities and their facility to acquire some or all literacy skills. Learning to read and write involves visual and auditory discrimination and memory, sequencing and practical awareness, eye/hand co-ordination and fine motor skills. A child with a weakness in one or more of these areas may experience considerable difficulty in becoming literate, and other areas of learning may also be affected. There may well be a family history of difficulties of this type.

The term **dyslexia** is often used to describe problems with learning to read and spell. However, many people prefer to use the term **specific learning difficulties** as it encompasses a wide range of problems and also makes it clear that various factors may lie at the root of the child's difficulties.

Identification

The most obvious sign that a person has dyslexia is that, unlike a slow learner, he or she makes markedly better progress in some areas of the curriculum than others.

Following is a list of some of the weaknesses a child may exhibit, but it is as well to remember that the pattern of difficulties will vary from child to child.

A child with specific learning difficulties/dyslexia may:

- confuse similar letters and words, either when spoken or written

- mispronounce words e.g. 'cobbler's club' for 'toddler's club'

- find it difficult to remember familiar words

- have problems in recalling facts learned by rote

- confuse letter/word order

- reverse letter and number, e.g. 15 for 51

- have difficulty tracking or focusing on words on the page, lose his or her place, or omit lines

- have difficulty in sequencing events, e.g. days of the week, essay planning

- experience difficulties in distinguishing direction, e.g. left/right, east/west, and in spatial awareness – including problems with the layout of work

- have poor co-ordination, e.g. with throwing, kicking, catching, skipping, or trip or fall over excessively

- have difficulty copying correctly, particularly from the blackboard

- read inaccurately

- have persistent difficulty in dressing and undressing, putting shoes on the correct feet – or be late in learning these skills

- have difficulty in clapping out rhythms

- have obvious 'good' and 'bad' days, for no apparent reason

- enjoy being read to, but show no interest in letters or words

- use substitute words or 'near-misses' e.g. 'lampshade' for 'lamp-post'

- mislabel – know colours but mislabel them e.g. 'black' for 'brown'

- have an early lisp

- not be able to remember the label for known objects e.g. table, chair

- confuse directional words e.g. up/down; in/out

- find difficulty with rhyming words e.g. 'cat'; 'mat'; 'sat'

- find difficulty in selecting the 'odd one out' e.g. 'cat'; 'mat'; 'pig'; 'fat'

- have difficulties with time sequence and getting things in chronological order (first for last, now for later)

- reverse the sequence of words or form (*there once was* for *once there was*, was/saw, out/not) or reverse the concept (go/stop)

- be over-dependent on contextual clues

- mix upper and lower case letters e.g. 'BeTTer'

- show great difficulty in remembering whole-word patterns and not learn easily by the 'sight method'

- repeat speech errors in writing e.g. 'would of' for 'would have'

- have erratic handwriting and an inability to stay close to the margin

- confuse maths symbols and concepts.

Not all dyslexic children experience all of the difficulties listed above. Many very young children make similar mistakes to dyslexic children, so clues to identification are:

- the severity of the trait

- the clarity with which it may be observed

- the length of time during which it persists.

Your thoughts

Strategies

As children with dyslexia are weak in one or more channels of learning, a multi-sensory approach should be used wherever possible. This involves helping the child to learn by every available means: visual, auditory, spoken, tactile and kinaesthetic.

The advantage of a multi-sensory approach is that it enables the learner to use points of strength, while supporting weaker areas.

- Let the child know you are interested in his/her difficulties, and encourage him/her to ask for help.

- Make sure he or she is seated close enough to you to receive help easily.

- Give credit for ideas and content when marking work.

- Repeat new information and check that it has been understood.

- Allow sufficient time for work to be organised and completed.

- Teach study skills.

- Link spelling and handwriting in order to improve the motor memory.

- Encourage the use of the look/cover/write/check technique when spellings are being learned, and use finger tracing in the air or on the page.

- Teach spelling rules.

- Make use of mnemonics (e.g. because = **b**ig **e**lephants **c**annot **a**lways **u**se **s**mall **e**ntrances).

- Consider encouraging the child to use touch-typing to aid composition.

- Encourage the child to use the spell-checker on a word-processing package.

- Provide the child with a variety of ways of recording work (e.g. cassette tapes, charts, diagrams, word-processing).

- Use books with tapes to help with reading.

- Experiment with coloured filters if the child dislikes the glare of black print on white paper.

- Emphasise routine to help the child acquire a sense of organisation.

- Try to find something the child does well and give him/her a chance to shine. Give praise whenever possible.

- Encourage dyslexic children to help in practical jobs.

- Do not:
  - assume the child is lazy or careless
  - compare him/her with the rest of the class
  - make him/her read aloud in class
  - correct every mistake
  - give long lists of spellings
  - insist on rewriting, unless there is a definite purpose
  - spoil every experience by making him/her write about it
  - ridicule untidy writing.

With very young children, saying nursery rhymes together, reading poems, making up jingles and limericks, mime, drama, talking about pictures, using action games, using board games to develop turn-taking, playing pairs, Pelmanism or other memory games, clapping out syllables, and singing songs involving memory and sequencing, may all be helpful.

Help children to learn to follow instructions by starting with only one or two – 'please pick up the pencil and put it in the box'. Gradually make the sequence longer – 'go to the shelf, find the red box, bring it to me'. Encourage the child to repeat the instruction before carrying it out.

Some of the following strategies may also help.

- Encourage the child to practice physical skills such as throwing, catching, kicking balls, skipping, hopping, jumping and balancing.

- Encourage large writing movements (e.g. as part of music and/or movement lessons), or by using the forefinger with materials such as sand.

- Talk about books, using the language of books – pictures, words and letters – to realise that books can be looked at, read and enjoyed over and over again.

- Show how to hold a book, which way it opens, where the story starts, where the top of the page is and in which direction the words flow.

DYSPRAXIA AND DEVELOPMENTAL CO-ORDINATION DISORDER/DELAY (DCD)

Definition

Dyspraxia is a difficulty in the way the brain processes information, which results in messages not being properly or fully transmitted. It affects the co-ordination of movement, perception and thought, and is a difficulty in formulating the plan rather than a primary problem of motor execution.

If a child's performance in daily activities requiring motor co-ordination is significantly below that expected given his/her age and measured intelligence, he or she may have developmental co-ordination disorder/delay (DCD).

Identification

Dyspraxia/DCD may be shown by marked delays in achieving motor milestones (e.g. crawling or walking), dropping things, difficulties with balance, 'clumsiness', or poor performance in sports or handwriting. Affected children may have problems using knives and forks, tying shoelaces or holding a pencil. When hand writing, they may also show difficulties with directionality and pressure on the page.

Visual and perceptual difficulties (with copying from the board, or following sequential instructions for example) can also be symptoms of dyspraxia/DCD.

Strategies

An occupational therapist should assess the child and suggest activity ideas and strategies to encourage development and limit the impact of difficulties both in school and at home. The child should possibly attend a treatment group and his or her progress should be closely monitored and regulary reviewed. The following strategies may also help.

- Giving clear and unambiguous instructions.

- Breaking down activities into small steps.

- Arranging a 'buddy system'.

- Allowing extra time for completing work.

- Teaching the child strategies for remembering things.

Your thoughts

Useful organisations

British Institute of Learning Difficulties

Campion House
Green Street
Kidderminster DY10 1JL
Tel: 01562 723 010
Fax: 01562 723 029
E-mail: enquiries@bild.org.uk
Web: www.bild.org.uk

Provides services that promote good practice in the provision and planning for people with learning disabilities.

Equals

PO Box 107
North Shields
Tyne and Wear NE30 2YG
Tel/fax: 0191 272 8600
E-mail: admin@equals.co.uk
Web: www.equals.co.uk

National organisation for teachers of pupils with learning difficulties within special school and mainstream education.

The British Dyslexia Association

98 London Road
Reading
Berkshire RGI 5AU
Tel: 0118 966 2677
Fax: 0118 935 1927
Helpline: 0118 966 8271
Web: www.bda-dyslexia.org.uk
E-mail: info@dyslexiahelp-bda.demon.co.uk.

Offers advice, information and help to dyslexic people and their families, and to professionals.

The Dyslexia Institute

133 Gresham Road
Staines
Middlesex TW18 2AJ
Tel: 01784 463 851
Fax: 01784 460 747
E-mail: info@dyslexia-inst-org.uk
Web: www.dyslesxia-inst.org.uk

Offers assessment and teaching for people with dyslexia, and training for teachers.

The Dyspraxia Foundation

8 West Alley
Hitchin
Hertfordshire SG5 1EG
Tel: 01462 455016
Fax: 01462 455052
Helpline: 01462 454986
Web: www.dyspraxiafoundation.org.uk

Exists to support individuals affected by dyspraxia and their families.

The Down's Syndrome Association

155 Mitcham Road
London SW17 9PG
Tel: 020 8682 4001
Fax: 020 8682 4012
Web: www.dsa-uk.com

Provides information about Down's Syndrome to those with a professional interest, as well as supporting people affected by the condition, and their families.

MENCAP (Royal Society for Mentally Handicapped Children and Adults)

123 Golden Lane
London EC1Y 0RT
Tel: 020 7454 0454
Fax: 020 7696 5540
E-mail: information@mencap.org.uk
Web: www.mencap.org.uk

MENCAP Cymru

31 Lambourne Crescent
Cardiff Business Park
Cardiff CF14 5GF
Tel: 029 2074 7588
Fax: 029 2074 7550
E-mail: information.wales@mencap.org.uk

MENCAP Northern Ireland

Segal House
4 Annadale Ave
Belfast BT7 3JH
Tel: 02090 091 351
Fax: 02890 640 121
E-mail: mencapni@mencap.org.uk

Works with people with a learning disability to fight discrimination against them.

2

SENSORY AND PHYSICAL IMPAIRMENTS

As children with a sensory or physical impairment may be dependent on others for some of their needs, it is important that they have opportunities to excel at something. Aim to allow each child to emerge in his/her own right so that he or she is not seen just as someone who is 'disabled'. Give him or her every chance to join in, to express opinions and to interact with the peer group.

Whatever the sensory or physical difficulty involved, the first support strategy for a teacher or teaching assistant to adopt is to become as well-informed as possible. Read any medical or other records the school holds, and then find out who is available to help.

General points

Mobility

If a child has difficulty getting about, the school will need to assess the extent to which classrooms and corridors are wheelchair friendly. Issues to consider include:

- the layout of the classroom (aim to maximise space)

- the position of the child in the classroom – are resources accessible to him or her?

- the best route from one area of the school to another (the shortest route may not be the easiest)

- the time the child needs to get from one area to another

- whether another child should be asked to help push a wheelchair (if the user does not control it) or be available to lend a hand or carry a bag, etc

- if the child has a wheelchair, if he or she can transfer in and out of it – e.g. to sit at a desk, or lie on a PE mat.

A note on lifting

Remember that lifting a child is not as easy as it looks when done by an expert. Unless you have been properly trained, do not risk being injured yourself. Make sure you always have sufficient help on hand if lifting is necessary.

If it is important that the child maintains a good sitting position, ask health professionals whether there is a local seating clinic that can help.

A note on administering medication

There are no national guidelines for schools or teachers on giving medication to pupils. Teachers have a general duty to act **in loco parentis**, but they are not contractually obliged either to administer medicines or to supervise pupils taking them. If they choose to administer medicine, they should have appropriate training. For more information and advice, contact the Association of Teachers and Lecturers to request the information sheet 'Administering **medication to pupils**'.

A note on hand control

If a child's hand control is weak, consider using:

- jumbo pencils, wax crayons, thick felt pens, paintbrushes held in the teeth or velcro-ed to the hand

- non-slip mats or even sellotape to hold paper, books, plates etc in place

- foam rubber around cutlery handles

- rimmed, rather than flat plates

- specially-adapted computer switches and concept keyboards

- different ways of recording work, such as word-processing, talking into a tape-recorder, and dictating to a friend.

Working towards independent learning

Almost inevitably, some children with serious sensory and/or physical impairments will be highly dependent on others. It is therefore all the more important to create opportunities for some degree of independence in terms of learning as well as living. Give the child time and opportunity to initiate and/or complete an activity he or she is carrying out as independently as possible. If the child has a dedicated teaching assistant, he or she should step back occasionally to facilitate this. Opportunities for the child to be amongst his/her peers, independent of the assistant, should also be encouraged.

Always be on the lookout for informal as well as formal opportunities for recognising achievement.

Hearing impairment

Hearing impairment has been described by some people as a 'hidden' special educational need, because it is not always immediately obvious but its effects can lead to misunderstanding and confusion.

Definition

There are very few people who are unable to hear any sounds at all – a hearing loss may range from a very slight impairment to profound deafness. An estimated one in four children under the age of seven have, at some time, suffered from a hearing loss of some kind. There will be different degrees of loss, and it may affect one ear, or both ears. Whatever the hearing loss, the acquisition of language and development of communication skills are vital if a child is to have access to information and receives his/her educational entitlement. This can be achieved through an oral/aural, total communication or bilingual approach.

There are two main types of hearing loss, **conductive** and **sensori-neural**.

Anything which interferes with the transmission of sound from the outer to the inner ear will result in a conductive loss of hearing. The interference may arise from congestion in or damage to the ear/s, and it may be temporary or permanent. An infection can cause fluid in the middle ear cavity, leading to what is known as 'glue ear'. Glue ear can cause a delay in acquiring literacy skills because sounds are heard indistinctly. If symptoms do not clear up within a few months, a referral to an ear, nose and throat specialist or an audiologist may be necessary. In persistent cases of glue ear, grommets are inserted to help drain off the fluid.

Conductive hearing loss causes sounds to be muted – a normal speaking voice may sound like a whisper. Depending on its cause, it may be treated or alleviated by medicine, surgery or electrical aids. While hearing aids can be helpful, as the volume of all speech sounds is amplified, background noise will be amplified as well.

As it is caused by damage to the mechanism of the inner ear, sensori-neural loss of hearing is less common, but more likely to be permanent. While it can result in a hearing loss similar to conductive deafness, it generally results in sounds becoming distorted, because some sounds are heard but not others. For instance, a high frequency loss will affect the person's ability to hear most of the consonants. Speech will sound like a series of vowel sounds, and word endings – which indicate plurals and tenses – will be missing. Less common is low frequency loss, which affects a child's ability to hear vowels.

Hearing aids, while beneficial, will not enable a person to hear the missing sounds so the distortion will still be there – they will not restore normal hearing in the way that glasses correct sight. Children with sensori-neural loss find it harder to acquire speech, and their language development may be delayed.

Cochlear implants are relatively new but are being used with more and more children. A prosthesis is worn partly inside the body and partly outside, and is used to aid hearing.

Identification

Older children with any degree of hearing loss should have had their condition identified at an earlier stage, but it is easy for younger children to escape detection and to be labelled as slow, lazy or inattentive. This is particularly true of children with conductive hearing loss, which may fluctuate from day to day and cause adults to remark that 'they can hear when they want to'.

Sensori-neural loss is being detected at a much younger age as Universal Neonatal Hearing Screening is adopted in more regions. This identifies any possible hearing impairment within days of birth. Children with a significant loss will have impaired speech; this will be apparent in the flatness of their intonation, the absence of certain sounds, or the omission of words that are less important for conveying meaning. Speech therapy and 'audiology trawling' may help address this problem. However, children with a less significant impairment, but one that may nonetheless affect their progress, can all too easily slip through the net.

Watch out, then, for the child who:
- is slow to react

- is the last to follow instructions

- watches others' reactions and then copies

- is always coming to check what he or she should be doing

- has a friend who helps and lets him/her copy work

- seems to be day-dreaming

- is tense and over-anxious

- watches faces intently

- turns his/her head to one side when listening

- can't locate the source of a sound

- keeps saying 'what' or 'pardon'

- tires easily when working

- finds it hard to hear when there is a great deal of background noise, e.g. in the dining room

- finds it hard to follow discussions

- has poor language development

- can't regulate his/her voice – either shouts or whispers

- finds some sounds difficult to pronounce, particularly 's', 'sh' and 't'

- changes topic abruptly when conversing

- finds oral work harder than written

- takes expressions such as 'I'm pulling your leg' literally

- has tantrums due to frustration

- has aggressive outbursts

- has problems socially.

Strategies

All hearing-impaired children will lip-read to some extent. This takes a great deal of concentration, as does the effort to follow what is being said. Teachers and teaching assistants should therefore keep activities short and make allowances if the child tires towards the end of the day. Check whether he or she is supposed to wear a hearing aid and find out about the particular type of aid by asking the parent or advisory/specialist teacher. Providing a radio aid may also help.

Following are other strategies that can make a real difference.

- Speak clearly but do not shout, over-pronounce or exaggerate your words.

- Cut down on background noise e.g. by having chairs with rubber stoppers.

- Seat the child near the front of the class, on the window side of the room, so that the light falls on your face.

- Try to seat the child away from sources of noise – traffic, noisy heaters, the hum of the OHP.

- Don't talk while writing on the blackboard – when speaking, try to look in the direction of the child.

- Do use animated facial expressions and point to sources of information.

- Don't use single words – help the child by providing the context.

- Do use visual support e.g. objects, pictures, photos.

- Keep your hands and any visual aids away from your mouth.

- Speak naturally, at a normal speed (unless you normally speak very fast, in which case try to slow down).

- If the child doesn't understand, don't repeat what has been said, but do try to rephrase it.

Your thoughts

- Make sure the child is paying attention before you start speaking.

- If using a radio, cassette player or TV, give the child some indication beforehand of what the programme is about; if necessary, provide a transcript. Pause when convenient to summarise what has happened so far and reinforce any new vocabulary.

- Develop listening skills by playing auditory discrimination games (e.g. identifying instruments) and auditory memory games, e.g. 'I went shopping and bought…'

- Make sure the child is included in group discussions – place him/her with others who will be sympathetic, and allow him/her time both to follow what is said and to contribute.

- Remember class discussions are particularly hard to follow, so repeat children's contributions.

- Be aware that it is impossible to lip-read and to take notes at the same time – provide notes, or ask another adult or child to help with note-taking.

- Realise that older children will need help with mastering the technical language of a range of subjects. New terms, acronyms or familiar words used in a new context should be written out and then explained.

- If a child uses sign language and has an interpreter, speak directly to the child and not the adult (interpreting is extremely wearing and there will be a need for frequent breaks).

- Make sure instructions about homework are understood – by getting the child to repeat what he or she is to do, for example.

- Encourage the child to indicate when he or she has not understood, as it is important for him or her to take increasing responsibility for his/her learning.

A child with a hearing loss has to work extra hard to reach his/her potential and to be accepted socially. Be sympathetic, offer encouragement and do everything you can to ensure that other children realise that being deaf does not mean that the individual is any less intelligent than others or does not have language. Latch on to the child's strengths and provide opportunities where he or she can shine.

Visual impairment

Definition

Visual impairment is a low incidence condition affecting approximately two children per thousand. There are many causes of blindness and partial sight and the effect of particular conditions is unique to the individual. The broadest definition is that vision can be considered to be impaired if, even with the use of contact lenses or glasses, a person's sight cannot be fully corrected.

Very few people can see nothing at all. Some may be able to perceive light and be able to use this information to know where a window is, or a light source and be able to orientate themselves in a room. For some people, a visual impairment will mean that they can see up to a certain distance. Others may have a reduced field of vision and may only be able to see objects held directly in front or to one side. Some people will see blurred images, for others what they see appears to be constantly 'dancing up and down', others may have patches of vision which 'disappear', or difficulty perceiving depth and perspective. Some colours may be easier to see, with others being effectively indistinguishable or invisible. Some people may be able to see fine detail close up, but others may be able to perceive bold outlines, but not details.

A child who has little or no vision from birth will need more help to understand visual concepts than a child who has previously had some sight.

Some children may have more minor sight difficulties, perhaps colour blindness or a squint in one eye, or a lazy eye. These may have only a limited effect on their learning and may not warrant individual education plans. However, if there is any doubt about a child's vision, it should be thoroughly investigated and assessed. The first person to contact is one of your LEA's qualified teachers of visually impaired children.

More than half of children who have impaired vision have additional special educational needs. Where this is the case, the totality of the individual's needs must be addressed by a multi-disciplinary team of health, education and social work professionals.

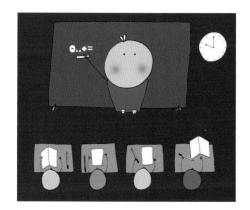

Identification

Most children with a visual impairment are diagnosed before they reach school age. However, some children slip through the net, others develop a sight difficulty during their school years and those who are known to have a visual impairment may also experience difficulties if their sight deteriorates further.

The following are potential indicators of a visual difficulty. If in doubt, it is best for the child's vision to be assessed.

Watch out for the child who:
- has watery, itchy or inflamed eyes
- keeps blinking rapidly or rubbing his or her eyes
- frowns, squints, or peers at work
- tilts the head, or holds work at an odd angle or distance
- closes or covers one eye when looking at books
- turns the head to follow the line across the page when reading
- appears clumsy
- bumps into people or objects
- has difficulty throwing, kicking and catching
- finds difficulty in copying from the blackboard or from a book
- confuses letters of similar appearance, such as c, e, a, o
- writes in large letters and not on the line
- presses hard with a pencil or pen
- uses a finger to keep his or her place on the page
- misses out words and lines when reading
- complains that worksheets are too faint
- complains that he or she can't see the blackboard
- has difficulty setting out sums
- dislikes strong light or glare
- complains of frequent headaches
- works slowly
- has a short attention span.

Your thoughts

Strategies

Assessing what a child can see in different conditions (for example in a well-lit room, in a corridor without natural light, outside in bright sunshine) is a complex skill. The assessment needs to encompass what a child can see and how he or she uses his/her vision. A qualified teacher of children with impaired vision should conduct a functional vision assessment and advise on how the child's educational needs should be met.

Such advice should include:

- guidance on teaching methods

- advice about the presentation and modification of learning materials

- information about how the child will read, obtain information, and write – for example, using Braille, typing or handwriting

- recommendations of special equipment including computer technology

- recommendations of specialist learning resources

- advice on classroom management

- arrangements for national curriculum assessments and other examinations.

Get as much information as possible from the child, his/her parents and the advisory teacher. Find out if the child is supposed to wear glasses, and if so when. The advisory teacher should also explain other visual aids the child might need (for example magnifiers) and whether worksheets, maps or diagrams should be presented in a particular way.

Much depends on the degree and type of visual impairment. With appropriate support, partially sighted and blind children can and do succeed in the mainstream classroom.

The following strategies for using sighted and non-sighted methods of learning may help.

- There may be an optimum place for the child to sit in the classroom (e.g. in good light, away from glare, near a power point, at a particular distance and angle from the blackboard).

- Visually impaired people do not have extraordinary powers of hearing. On the contrary, a visually impaired person needs help to identify, locate and interpret sounds to make sense of what is happening. For this reason, unnecessary noise in the classroom should be minimised and, where appropriate, sounds explained as they occur.

- When addressing the child, use his/her name first to get attention (this equates to eye contact). This enables a visually impaired child to know when he or she is receiving praise or instructions and when it is appropriate to ignore comments directed at others.

- Use descriptive language – 'it is to the left of the bookcase' is more useful than 'over there'.

- Keep the classroom tidy so that a visually impaired child doesn't knock into objects or trip on bags or toys. Always remember to inform the child if furniture has been moved around, and allow him/her time to familiarise him/herself with the new layout.

- Use a heavy black pen, which is clearer to read than pencil.

- Find out which colour contrast suits the child. Black writing on a white matt surface makes effective contrast without glare, although black on yellow is sometimes better.

- On worksheets, provide clear lines for the child to write on. Avoid cluttering pages of worksheets with illustrations and italic or ornate fonts. Lower case text is easier to read than capital letters.

- Cut out unnecessary detail on diagrams, and enhance with colour if that is helpful.

- Learn how to make tactile diagrams, simplifying detail and introducing contrasting textures, labelling in Braille if appropriate. In each case consider whether a diagram is the best way to communicate the information.

- Make outlines clear and bold.

- Allow time for writing and let the learner record some work orally (e.g. using a tape recorder).

- Allow extra time for reading print or Braille and for the acquisition of any specialist skills such as touch typing, mobility, learning Braille and pre-Braille activities.

- Find out if the child has an optimum length of time during which he or she can work efficiently and effectively – reading print with impaired vision often causes fatigue, and reading in Braille requires great concentration.

- Make use of word-processing, both to assist the child in the presentation of his or her own work and also to prepare learning materials. Experiment with different font styles and sizes to find out which are easiest for an individual partially sighted child to read. Often enlarging the text to 16 point or 18 point can help. Braillists can also use computer translation packages to create Braille and print versions.

- Use computer technology to give children greater access to printed work and to CD-ROMs.

- Record large amounts of text onto cassette.

- Magnify books and worksheets if necessary, but remember the enlarged version will take longer to scan, and that the child will see fewer words at one time. The text may need reformatting to keep the page size manageable.

- Dictate as you write on the blackboard. Some children may find a paper copy helpful.

- Go over classroom displays, explaining them in detail, so that the child can enjoy them for further learning. If a child's work is in Braille, put a print version with it so that other children can read it.

- Use a multi-sensory approach – allow children to handle, smell and look closely at objects. Involve a visually impaired learner with practical demonstrations such as science experiments.

- Encourage the child with impaired vision to make full use of any low vision aids recommended by the advisory teacher, such as magnifiers.

- So as to maximise the child's independence, refer to an orientation and mobility officer for advice to ensure that the classroom is organised, structured and accessible.

- Label equipment in large print or Braille where appropriate.

- Obtain specialist equipment such as tactile rulers, heavy-lined stationery, and talking calculators. Keep in touch with new services, equipment and developments and seek advice from curriculum specialists.

- Negotiate extra time for preparing individual learning materials and for liaising with specialists such as a teacher of visually impaired children or a mobility specialist.

- Contact other teachers with experience of teaching your subject area to children with impaired vision through curriculum groups supported by **RNIB** (see Useful organisations on page 38).

- Develop a whole school approach to understanding visual impairment and its implications for teachers, teaching assistants and children.

A child with a sight problem may be over-protected by other children, ignored by them or excluded from social activities. Try to help the peer group to appreciate the child's whole personality and not define him/her only as 'someone with a sight problem'. Use the child's strengths and encourage him or her to be as independent as possible.

Deafblindness/multi-sensory impairment

Definition

Deafblindness is a combination of both hearing and sight impairment. It does not necessarily mean the total loss of both senses – indeed the majority of deafblind people do have some degree of residual hearing and/or sight. Those with a severe degree of both sight and hearing impairment may also be referred to as having a multi-sensory impairment or loss.

A person is regarded as deafblind or multi-sensory impaired when the combination of his or her two sensory impairments intensify the impact of each other, and prevent the individual functioning as fully as a blind or partially-sighted person who can hear, or a deaf or hard-of-hearing person who can see.

A precise definition of deafblindness is difficult because the degrees of deafness and blindness, possibly combined with different degrees of other disabilities, are not uniform and the educational needs of the affected child therefore have to be decided on an individual basis.

Identification

Deafblind children will find it difficult to utilise, and benefit fully from, educational support for deaf people or blind people – meeting their needs therefore requires a separate approach.

In particular, deafblind children experience problems with:

- the development of communication skills – to a degree that they require adapted or augmented forms of communication

- mobility – they may need specialised learning programmes and modifications to their environment (e.g. a multi-sensory room)

- integrating information received through other senses – as a result, they may require individual activity-based programmes that have been differentiated to meet their specific needs

- social interaction and the development of independence skills – they may need positive interaction on the part of the teacher/teaching assistant, and specific curricular programmes.

Congenitally deafblind children are born with a dual sensory loss and often develop additional and/or multiple disabilities, including learning disabilities.

Some deafblind people develop their dual sensory loss later in life – children with 'Usher Syndrome' for example are born deaf or hard of hearing, then gradually start to lose their sight in late childhood.

Your thoughts

Strategies

The needs of deafblind/multi-sensory impaired children vary considerably, and cannot be assumed or generalised. In many cases, an individual, needs-led approach to their education is necessary. The following points suggest key areas that should to be considered.

Curriculum

- An individual curriculum, based on an individual assessment of educational and social needs, is required to ensure all the needs of the child are met, including communication needs, access to information, mobility and social skills.

- Deafblind awareness training and development is necessary for all school staff and other pupils in the class. The postgraduate qualification in multi-sensory impairment facilitated by the **University of Birmingham** may be appropriate for staff.

An adapted physical environment

- Classrooms need to be well lit to facilitate lip-reading, following sign language, reading and mobility. Overhead fluorescent strip lighting is best.

- Light, plain floor coverings and medium to dark furnishings are helpful. Colour and texture differences will help children to differentiate their surrounding environment and aid visual communication and independent mobility.

- Carpeted rooms are preferable as they tend to be quieter and reduce echoing. Avoid using rooms next to busy roads or other noisy environments.

- Induction loops may be necessary for hearing aid users.

- Consider providing mobility trails.

Communication needs

A school-wide policy on communication is essential to enable the deafblind child to be integrated into the school's physical and social environment. The communication needs of the child will be highly individual.

There are many different forms of communication including:

- total communication – e.g. the use of voice, objects of reference, textured communication, symbols, pictures, etc

- finger spelling, deafblind manual or block

- visual sign language – e.g. British Sign Language (BSL) or hands on signing

- lip reading

- portable communication aids – e.g. light writers.

A one-to-one staff/child ratio is needed. **Intervenors** are support assistants who help the deafblind child to access learning opportunities. They have a range of communication skills and knowledge of alternative methods of communication.

Specialist aids

- CCTV, large print, audiotapes, computer disks and technical support aids and textured communication – e.g. Braille, Moon may all be helpful.

- Communication by computer disk is increasingly popular. It is, of course, only useful in schools if the child has access to a computer with Braille display, speech synthesisers or large character software.

- Braille printers, text phones, scanners, and induction loop systems should be considered.

Social needs

Deafblindness is a low-incidence disability, which by its very nature is isolating. The social needs of the child are therefore an important element in his/her educational needs. Mobility, environmental awareness, socialising and communicating with fellow children need constant consideration.

A communicator guide is someone who acts as the eyes and ears of the deafblind person to enable two-way communication and to interpret in informal situations – shopping, socialising, and accessing services like banks and post offices, for example.

Physical impairment

This section covers a wide range of physical and medical conditions. Some children with a physical disability will be easily identifiable, but others less so if their condition can be effectively controlled. Medical conditions which affect children's stamina and therefore their ability to participate fully in all aspects of the curriculum are also considered here. Some physical disabilities have allied medical conditions which require regular medication, sometimes to be taken during school hours.

Children with some medical conditions are at an extra disadvantage if their absences are frequent enough to get in the way of their learning. Home learning programmes can be helpful, although time-consuming for the teacher who oversees them.

Some physical and medical problems are congenital; others emerge later on. Schools need to know enough about children's medical conditions to help them access their educational entitlement.

Finding the information you need to support a child's education

If the child has a statement, then the statement itself may be a valuable starting point.

If not:

- consult your colleagues

- look at any records from the previous school

- talk to the child and his/her family

- make contact with your local SEN adviser, advisory teachers, and support teams

- seek information from special school colleagues if you are in a mainstream school

- consider arranging a meeting with the school doctor/nurse/therapist.

Following are some of the questions you might need to ask.

- Is the child on medication and, if so, does the drug affect his/her capacity to learn?

- Is the child likely to have frequent absences from school? If so, do you need to set work to be done at home?

- How far does the disability limit participation in school life? For instance, can the child go out to play regardless of the weather; participate in PE, games and other activities; go on school trips? Can she or he go swimming?

- What can the child do independently?

- When should I offer help?

When you have collected the information you need, plan how you will overcome or modify any potential problems.

HEREDITARY PROBLEMS
Cystic fibrosis

Cystic fibrosis is the UK's most common life-threatening inherited disease among Caucasians (people of Indo-European origin). It occurs in approximately 1 in 2,500 children.

Children with cystic fibrosis can have gastro-intestinal problems resulting from a damaged pancreas. This is caused by the presence of thick mucus, which is characteristic of cystic fibrosis and which affects other organs, notably the lungs.

At the beginning of the twentieth century, children with cystic fibrosis did not live very long, but the discovery of powerful antibiotics and other effective treatments such as physiotherapy and dietary care now mean that most children with cystic fibrosis live into adulthood with a manageable degree of disability.

Identification

The most noticeable feature of cystic fibrosis is a non-infective persistent cough. For the affected child, this may be embarrassing in front of other children, especially as a severe attack of coughing sometimes leads to coughing up mucus, or vomiting.

The main digestive problem caused by cystic fibrosis is a malfunctioning of the pancreas. (The pancreas is a gland that produces insulin, regulating the amount of sugar in the blood. It also produces digestive juices or enzymes, which pass into the intestine where they aid the digestion and absorption of food.)

Children with cystic fibrosis may be more prone to sinusitis, hay fever, arthritis, diabetes, heart strain and cirrhosis of the liver, but these are fairly rare complications which usually develop in older children or adults. Most children with cystic fibrosis respond to childhood diseases in the same way as their non-affected peers but they do run a slightly higher risk of chicken-pox pneumonitis, and some children may need to be withdrawn from school if there is an outbreak of chicken-pox.

Other complications are the possibility of delayed sexual maturity and probable future sterility for boys with cystic fibrosis.

Your thoughts

Strategies

Children with cystic fibrosis are as academically able as their peers, and teachers should expect the same standards. They may, however, be absent from school for significant periods because of chest infections or hospitalisation, and so will require extra help to catch up with the rest of the class.
If a child is not seriously ill, work can be set for him/her to complete at home or in hospital.

Some older children use portable intravenous antibiotic equipment which means they can attend their normal lessons but cannot cope with the rough and tumble of the playground.

Physical exercise is extremely beneficial to children with cystic fibrosis, so full participation in PE lessons is likely if a child is well. Sympathetic understanding is required though for times when a child is tired and lacks energy after a cold or chest infection.

Many children with cystic fibrosis learn from an early age to administer their own antibiotics and set up their nebulisers. School staff who find the whole prospect alarming may be reassured by the matter of fact way in which these children carry out their daily routine. If you need information and advice about administrating medicines to a child, please refer to page 17. You could also contact the Association of Teachers and Lecturers for the Association's information sheet 'Administering medication to pupils'.

Haemophilia

Haemophilia is a disorder affecting blood coagulation. In severe cases, minor injuries cause severe bleeding and spontaneous bleeding in vital organs. In less severe cases, severe bleeding occurs only after major injury. Treatment is by injection of 'Factor VIII'.

With treatment, haemophiliacs can lead normal lives, but dangerous and/or contact sports should be avoided. Parents should always be consulted about how best to manage their child's education and care during school hours.

Sickle cell anaemia

Sickle cell anaemia is so called because of the sickle shape of the red blood cells. This is caused by abnormal haemoglobin, which results in increased viscosity of the blood, thereby obstructing blood flow. In the UK, it is most common in people of Afro-Caribbean descent.

School staff should be aware that people affected by sickle cell anaemia can experience severe pain. The sickle cells are more fragile than normal cells, have a shorter life and so cause anaemia.

Parents should be consulted about how best to manage their child's education and care during school hours.

CONGENITAL CONDITIONS

Cerebral palsy

Cerebral palsy affects around 1 in 400 people. It occurs when part of the brain is not working properly or has not developed properly – this happens either before birth, at birth or during early childhood. It is permanent but non-progressive and affects the individual's ability to control his/her movements. It can affect mobility but may also affect speech and communication, manipulation, vision, hearing, perception, cognition and/or eating and drinking. Epilepsy is sometimes also present.

Types of cerebral palsy include spastic (involving stiffened muscles and decreased joint movement), athetoid (involving involuntary muscle movement and problems controlling the tongue, breathing and vocal chords), and ataxic (involving difficulties with balance, shaky hand movements and jerky speech).

How well a child succeeds in education will depend on the degree of severity and whether there are other learning difficulties present – e.g. in the ability to concentrate. The child may have regular therapy and/or may attend intensive courses at different centres, for example, at The Bobath Centre or at Peto UK. He or she may, therefore, be occasionally absent from school.

Limb deformities

The tragic side-effects of the drug thalidomide focused public attention on the problems faced by people with limb deformities. Although the drug is no longer used, limb deformities still occur and may affect the development of one or more limbs.

An affected child might have a prosthesis and may require help to change it, depending on the activity taking place. He or she may have a wheelchair or walking aid. As the child grows, the prosthesis will need to be changed and this will mean that he or she will be absent from lessons. The child may experience some soreness as he or she gets used to the new prosthesis.

Spina bifida and hydrocephalus

Spina bifida – literally meaning 'split spine' – is a condition where a child is born with a defect in the formation of the spine. There are various types of spina bifida and, while some children are severely disabled, others have the condition in only a minor form.

As a teacher or teaching assistant, you need to be aware of some of the implications for a child with spina bifida. He or she may have limited or no sensation below the spinal lesion, and so fail to notice cuts and bruises. To prevent burns, for example, ensure the child knows if a radiator is on. As the child gets older, he or she will take more responsibility for him/herself.

Many children with spina bifida also have hydrocephalus (water on the brain) and need a shunt to rectify this. A child whose shunt becomes blocked or damaged may become seriously ill, so you need to be aware of the signs. Information can be obtained from the Association for Spina Bifida and Hydrocephalus (ASBAH) – for contact details, please refer to page 40.

Strategies

- Use a buddy system.

- Talk to parents.

- Make use of audio-visual aids.

- Think about curriculum access – allowing extra time, teaching styles, and appropriate support.

OTHER CONDITIONS
Accidental injuries
If a child suffers a serious accident which results in permanent or long-term disability, he or she will need to learn to adapt to a different lifestyle – emotionally as well as in terms of his/her physical abilities. For example, a child who has suffered a permanent spinal injury due to a road traffic accident may require a wheelchair. The whole class may require some form of support or counselling when a friend and peer has suffered such a severe trauma.

Allergies
An allergy is an adverse reaction, caused by a hypersensitivity to a substance.

Allergies generally cause problems in one of three ways.

1 Intestinal allergies may cause vomiting, abdominal pain and diarrhoea.

2 Skin allergies may show as a red skin rash, a 'nettle rash' or dermatitis.

3 Respiratory allergies may result in asthma or hay fever.

Treatment
- Try to recognise the problem.
- Advise the child to see his or her doctor.
- Seek immediate medical aid if necessary.

Anaphylactic shock
Anaphylactic shock is the name given to a rare, generalised and dangerous allergic reaction which requires urgent medical attention. It is a massive allergic reaction within the body.

Sensitive individuals may develop this reaction to:
- the injection of a particular drug
- the eating of a particular food – e.g. peanuts, or other nuts
- the sting of a particular insect – e.g. a bee, or a wasp.

An anaphylactic shock will cause:
- substances to be released into the blood that dilate the blood vessels and constrict air passages
- a fall in blood pressure
- difficulty in breathing
- an increased risk of suffocation as the face and neck swell
- an urgent need for oxygen and a life-saving injection of adrenaline.

Symptoms displayed may include:
- widespread red, blotchy skin eruption
- anxiety
- swelling of the face and neck
- puffiness around the eyes
- impaired breathing
- a rapid pulse.

Treatment
- Seek immediate medical aid.
- Dial 999 for an ambulance or ensure that the child is taken urgently to a hospital.

Asthma

Asthma is a distressing condition in which an allergic reaction causes a narrowing of the tubes in the lungs, resulting in wheezing, coughing and shortness of breath. The trigger may be dust, pollen, fur or some other substance, certain foods, emotional upsets or physical exertion.

Affected children will have difficulty in breathing. They may also experience:

- wheezing when breathing out

- distress and anxiety

- difficulty speaking

- a blueness of the skin.

Treatment

An asthma attack can last for a few minutes or several hours.

- Help the child to sit down, encourage him/her to sit upright and lean forwards.

- Ensure a good supply of fresh air, and offer a drink of water.

- Regular asthma sufferers generally carry an inhaler – find it and encourage him/her to use it.

- Seek medical aid if necessary, especially if medication fails to relieve the attack in five to ten minutes.

- Reassure and calm the sufferer (but do not put your arm around him/her).

Eczema

Eczema is an allergy that results in an inflammation of the skin. Unless the itching is so intense that it affects concentration, or the condition so severe that it involves regular time off school, eczema should not cause educational difficulties.

Diabetes

Diabetes is a condition that causes the body to fail to regulate the concentration of sugar (glucose) in the blood. Diabetics are usually aware of their condition and are well prepared if the blood glucose level changes.

If the glucose level in the blood becomes too high or too low, a child may display some of the following symptoms:

- weakness, faintness or hunger

- palpitations and muscle tremors

- strange actions or behaviour

- sweating

- pallor and cold, clammy skin

- a strong, bounding pulse

- a deteriorating level of response

- shallow breathing.

Treatment

If the child is conscious, help him or her to sit or lie down, and give him or her a sugary drink, sugar lumps, chocolate or other sweet food, in order to raise the sugar content of the blood as quickly as possible. Seek medical aid.

If the child is unconscious, seek medical aid and stay with him/her. Remember to open his or her airway, check breathing and pulse (be prepared to resuscitate if necessary, if you have recent, appropriate training) and place the child in the recovery position.

Epilepsy

Epileptic fits are caused by an occasional sudden reaction of the nerve cells in the cortex of the brain. Seizures can be severe (causing loss of consciousness) or very mild (almost like daydreaming). Taken regularly, anti-convulsant drugs can suppress the fits. In some cases it is also possible to identify and then avoid factors which trigger attacks. Children with epilepsy can therefore take part in normal school activities, including swimming, as long as they are adequately supervised. In some cases, children will themselves recognise the warning signs of an impending fit.

One person in every 200 or so suffers from epilepsy and will be subject to fits or seizures. Epilepsy can occur at any age.

Symptoms of minor epilepsy include:
- sudden 'switching off', or 'daydreaming'
- staring blankly ahead
- slight twitching movements
- strange movements – e.g. making odd noises, or 'fiddling' with clothing
- no awareness that anything out of the ordinary has happened.

In cases of more severe epileptic fits, the child may:
- suddenly fall unconscious
- have a rigid and arching back
- have a blue tinge to the lips
- have breathing difficulties
- show convulsive movements.

Within a few minutes, the muscles will relax, breathing will return to normal and the child will return to consciousness.

Treatment

In cases of minor epilepsy:
- help the child to sit down in a quiet area and remove any possible source of harm
- talk calmly to the child, do not 'pester' him or her to recover
- stay with the child until he or she has recovered.

In cases of major epilepsy:
- protect the child from injury during the fit (make space around him/her and ask people to move away)
- loosen clothing around the neck and try to protect the head
- stay with the child until he or she has fully recovered
- seek immediate medical aid, if the seizure lasts longer than five minutes, if a second seizure quickly follows the first, or if the child is having trouble breathing.

Do not use force to restrain the child, place anything near his or her mouth, or attempt to lift or move him or her unless there is immediate danger.

Strategies

One of the most important factors in the impact of epilepsy upon children is the reactions of peers, family, and teachers or other professionals to the condition. Communicating positively and openly with children allows the epilepsy to become just another aspect of their lives. Educationally, a child with epilepsy can achieve as much as any other child who is not affected by the condition. Encouraging self-confidence and self-belief is one of the key ways in which schools can support affected children to fulfil their learning potential.

Some children with epilepsy may suffer from poor attention and confusion, memory problems, fatigue, poor processing abilities, irritability or behaviour problems. Encouraging a child with epilepsy to repeat information given may counter some periods of lost consciousness. The drug treatment for epilepsy can also have an adverse affect on the child, as it may cause behaviour difficulties, extreme tiredness, weight gain, hair loss and acne – all of which affect self confidence and ability to learn.

HIV and AIDS

HIV (Human Immunodeficiency Virus) is a virus that can damage the body's immune system. The immune system fights the virus and if the body's defences are severely weakened this can lead to AIDS (Acquired Immune Deficiency Syndrome). AIDS is the name of a collection of different diseases that can cause serious illness or death in both adults and children.

HIV is very fragile and is not easily transmitted. For example, it cannot survive in very hot water, in bleach or in detergent.

HIV is transmitted in three ways:

- through unprotected vaginal or anal intercourse

- by infected blood entering the blood stream (e.g. from a blood transfusion or from needle stick injuries)

- from a woman with HIV to her baby either during pregnancy, during delivery or from breast feeding.

There is no evidence that HIV can be caught from social contact. Hugging, touching and kissing, as well as being close to people, presents no risk of infection. HIV cannot be spread by: coughing, sneezing, sharing a toilet seat, sharing a drinking fountain, showers and swimming pools, sweat, tears and saliva, or animals and pets.

Confidentiality

There are special legal rules to protect the confidentiality of information held by the NHS. All local education authority staff, including school staff, have a legal duty to keep confidential all information which is given to them about a child's health.

Details of the HIV status of any child must not be passed on without the parent's or child's permission. This means that in most schools, staff will not know if a child is HIV positive. It is therefore essential that health and safety procedures for cleaning up blood and blood-stained body fluids are rigorously adhered to, and that disposable gloves are worn when bleeding children are treated.

Muscular dystrophy

Muscular dystrophy is the term for a group of diseases that involve a progressive degeneration of the muscles, particularly those affecting movement. The rate at which this occurs varies according to the form of the condition.

There are several inherited forms of the disease, one of which, Duchenne's, mainly affects boys. The commonest form in children affects particularly the upper part of the lower limbs. The child is clumsy, weak on his/her legs and has difficulty getting up after a fall. In another form, which begins usually about age 14, the muscles of the upper arm are first affected, spreading to the spine and lower limbs. In another, the face is first affected.

The severity of the condition varies greatly, as does the life expectancy of the affected person. There is no cure for muscular dystrophy, but therapy often helps to alleviate symptoms.

Schools can support children with muscular dystrophy by using a buddy system, fostering positive attitudes in others through PSHE, and considering any necessary improvements to classroom layouts and use of stairs.

Useful organisations

Hearing loss

National Deaf Children's Society (NDCS)
15 Dufferin Street
London EC1Y 8UR
Tel: 020 7490 8656
Fax: 020 7251 5020
E-mail: fundraising@ndcs.org.uk
Web: www.ndcs.org.uk

A charity dedicated to supporting deaf children, young deaf people and their families.

British Association of Teachers of the Deaf
21 The Haystacks
High Wycombe
Buckinghamshire HP13 6PY
E-mail: secretary@batod.org.uk
Web: www.batod.org.uk

Promotes the educational interests of all hearing-impaired children and young people, and represents the interests of their teachers.

British Deaf Association
1-3 Worship Street
London EC2A 2AB
Tel: 0870 770 3300
Fax: 020 7588 3527
E-mail: helpline@bda.org.uk
Web: www.bda.org.uk

British Deaf Association Wales
Shand House
2 Fitzalan Place
Cardiff CF24 0BE
Tel: 029 2030 2216
Fax: 029 2030 2218
E-mail: wales@bda.org.uk

British Deaf Association Northern Ireland
Wilton House, 3rd Floor
5-6 College Square
Belfast BT1 6AR
Tel: 028 9072 7400
Fax: 028 9072 7407
E-mail: northernireland@bda.org.uk

Works to build a strong and vibrant community of deaf people who use sign language, ensuring that they enjoy the same rights, responsibilities, opportunities and quality of life as everyone.

Royal National Institute for Deaf People (RNID)
19-23 Featherstone Street
London EC1Y 8SL
Tel: 020 7296 8000
Info line: 0808 808 0123
Fax: 020 7296 8199
E-mail: informationline@rnid.org.uk
Web: www.rnid.org.uk

Aims to achieve a better quality of life for deaf and hard of hearing people through information, training, education, research, campaigning and employment programmes.

Visually impaired

Royal National Institute for the Blind (RNIB)
105 Judd Street
London WC1H 9NE
Tel: 020 7388 1266
Helpline: 0845 766 9999
Fax: 020 7388 2034
E-mail: corpinfo@rnib.org.uk
Web: www.rnib.org.uk

RNIB Cymru
Trident Court
East Moors Road
Cardiff CF24 5TD
Tel: 029 2045 0440
Fax: 029 2044 9550

Helps people with sight problems with practical solutions to everyday challenges. Campaigns, promotes eye health and funds research.

Visual Impairment Centre for Teaching and Research
School of Education
University of Birmingham
Edgbaston
Birmingham B15 2TT
Tel: 0121 414 6733
E-mail: victar-enquiries@bham.ac.uk
Web: www.education.bham.ac.uk/research/victar

A research centre which also teaches and provides advice and resources in the area of visual impairment and education.

Deafblindness/multi-sensory impairment

Sense
11-13 Clifton Terrace
London N4 3SR
Tel: 020 7272 7774
Fax: 020 7272 6012
E-mail: enquiries@sense.org.uk
Web: www.sense.org.uk

Services and support for people who are deafblind or who have associated disabilities.

Deafblind UK
100 Bridge Street
Peterborough PE1 1DY
Tel: 01733 358 100
Helpline: 0800 132 320
Fax: 01733 358 356
E-mail: info@deafblinduk.org.uk
Web: www.deafblinduk.org.uk

Deafblind UK Northern Ireland Branch
Course Lodge
10 Coilhill Road
Killyleagh
Co.Down BT30 9ST
Tel: 028 4482 1983

Offers a range of services for deafblind people, including a helpline and specialist support.

Physical impairments

Disability Rights Commission
DRC Helpline
Freepost MID 02164
Stradford-upon-Avon CV37 9HY
Helpline: 08457 622 633
Fax: 08457 778 878
E-mail: enquiry@drc-gb.org
Web: www.drc-gb.org

Information and advice about all aspects of the Disability Discrimination Act, as well as signposting specialist organisations where necessary.

PHAB
Summit House
50 Wandle Road
Croydon CRO 1DF
Tel: 020 8667 9443
Fax: 020 8681 1399
E-mail: info@phabengland.org.uk
Web: www.phabengland.org.uk

Runs a national network of clubs for disabled people, offers residential holidays for young people and funds a variety of projects.

Cystic Fibrosis Trust
11 London Road
Kent BR1 1BY
Tel: 020 8464 7211
Fax: 020 8313 0472
Web: www.cftrust.org.uk

Provides advice and support for people affected by cystic fibrosis, and for their families.

The Haemophilia Society
Chesterfield House
385 Euston Road
London NW1 3AU
Tel: 0800 018 6068
Fax: 020 7387 8220
E-mail: info@haemophilia.org.uk
Web: www.haemophilia.org.uk

Offers information and advice on issues relating to haemophilia.

The Sickle Cell Society
54 Station Road
London NW10 4UA
Tel: 020 8961 7795
Fax: 020 8961 8346
E-mail: sickleinfo.line@btinternet.com
Web: www.sicklecellsociety.org

Information, caring and counselling for those with sickle cell disorders and their families.

Scope
6 Market Road
London N7 9PW
Helpline: 0808 800 3333
E-mail: cphelpline@scope.org.uk
Web: www.scope.org.uk

A disability organisation offering a range of services for people affected by cerebral palsy, including information and support.

The National Institute of Conductive Education
Cannon Hill House
Russell Road
Birmingham B13 8RD
Tel: 0121 449 1569
Fax: 0121 449 1611
E-mail: foundation@conductive-education.org.uk
Web: www.conductive-education.org.uk

Conductive Education is a form of special education and rehabilitation for children and adults with motor disorders.

Association for Spina Bifida and Hydrocephalus (ASBAH)
42 Park Road
Peterborough PE1 2UQ
Tel: 01733 555988
Fax: 01733 555985
E-mail: postmaster@asbah.org
Web: www.asbah.org

Offers advice, support and specialist services on all issues related to spina bifida and hydrocepahalus.

Other conditions
Headway – the brain injury association
Tel: 0115 924 0800
Fax: 0115 958 4446
E-mail: enquiries@headway.org.uk
Web: www.headway.org.uk

Provides information, support and services for people with brain injuries, and for their families and carers.

The Anaphylaxis Campaign
PO Box 275
Farnborough
Hampshire GU14 6XS
Tel: 01253 542 029
E-mail: info@anaphylaxis.org.uk
Web: www.anaphylaxis.org.uk

Information on anaphylaxis for anyone with an interest in the condition, including health and education professionals.

National Asthma Campaign
Providence House
Providence Place
London N1 0NT
Tel: 020 7226 2260
Helpline: 08457 01 02 03
Fax: 020 7704 0740
Web: www.asthmaplus.org.uk

Researches and campaigns on all aspects of asthma, as well as offering advice and information to those with an interest in the condition.

The National Eczema Society
Hill House
Highgate Hill
London NW19 5NA
Tel: 020 7281 3553
Helpline: 0870 241 3604
Fax: 020 7281 6395
Web: www.eczema.org

Works for people with eczema, dermatitis and sensitive skins.

Diabetes UK
10 Parkway
London NW1 7AA
Tel: 020 7424 1000
Fax: 020 7424 1001
E-mail: info@diabetes.org.uk
Web: www.diabetes.org.uk

Funds research, campaigns and helps people to live with diabetes.

National Centre for Young People with Epilepsy
St Piers Lane
Lingfield RH7 6PW
Tel: 01342 832243
Fax: 01342 834639
E-mail: info@ncype.org.uk
Web: www.ncype.org.uk

Provides specialist services for young people who have epilepsy.

National Society for Epilepsy
Chesham Lane
Chalfont St Peter
Bucks SL9 0RJ
Tel: 01494 601 300
Helpline: 01494 601 400
Fax: 01494 871 927
Web: www.epilepsynse.org.uk

Provides information, training and education about epilepsy as well as medical services.

The Terrence Higgins Trust
Nine offices in England and Wales
Helpline: 020 7242 1010
E-mail: info@tht.org.uk
Web: www.tht.org.uk

Offers services, support and information on HIV and AIDS.

Muscular Dystrophy Campaign
7/11 Prescott Place
London SW4 6BS
Tel: 020 7720 8055
Helpline: 020 7720 8055
Fax: 020 7498 0670
E-mail: info@muscular-dystrophy.org
Web: www.muscular-dystrophy.org
Northern Ireland Office
Tel/Fax 028 90 751497

Charity focusing on all muscular dystrophies and allied disorders. Pioneers the search for treatments and cures and provides practical, medical and emotional support to people affected by the condition.

There are many different kinds of speech and language difficulty, but all of them affect communication. Such difficulties may arise from an inability to cope with some aspect of the structure of language (phonological, grammatical or semantic), or with the way language is used to communicate. Children may exhibit problems with receptive language (processing the language they hear) and/or with expressive language (verbalising their thoughts and feelings).

Delayed and disordered development

Definition

There is a well-defined pattern of normal phonological and grammatical development, and a child with delayed language will go through the same stages of development – but at a slower rate. A child with a speech and language disorder however will deviate from the usual progression and exhibit abnormal development.

Phonological problems will be apparent in the way a child articulates sounds, syllables and words (sounds that are produced at the front of the mouth are commonly mastered before those at the back). Difficulties with grammar or syntax will show up in faulty word, phrase or sentence structure. (Young children learn to use single words to convey a complete thought, then two-word phrases.) Semantic problems may be either receptive (a child has difficulty understanding what is said) or expressive (a child is unable to convey meaning satisfactorily).

If the problem relates to using language rather than to the structure of language, the child has difficulty in using spoken language in a meaningful way. This may manifest itself in the child echoing what has been said, or not understanding either how to hold a conversation or to reply appropriately to questions.

Delayed language development may be due to an insufficiently stimulating environment, where a child is neither spoken to nor encouraged to speak. Conversely, an environment where there is constant noise and activity, but very little conversation, can also be detrimental. Disordered development is more likely to be the result of minimal brain damage, affecting a small but vital area of the brain. Physical abnormalities, such as a cleft palate, may lead to problems with articulation, while cognitive difficulties (see page 9) or hearing impairment (see page 18) can also delay the development of speech and language.

Identification

While problems with articulation are easy to spot, other difficulties may be less apparent. This is particularly as teachers become very skilled at interpreting what a child is trying to say and, in an effort to be helpful, don't always listen to what has actually been said. It is therefore important to notice how children respond to spoken language and how they use it themselves.

Watch out for:

- an inability to understand when addressed one-to-one, in a group situation, or when the whole class is addressed

- an inability to follow more than one, more than two, or more than three instructions, depending on age

- the use of one sound to cover two or more sounds, e.g. 'w' for both 'r' and 'w' (leading to 'wabbit' instead of 'rabbit')

- the use of a few sounds to cover a range of sounds, e.g. simplifying blends as in 'b' for 'br'

- muddling or simplifying words/phrases, e.g. 'winkipers' for windscreen wipers, 'par cark'

- a tendency to give one-word replies

- a tendency to avoid speaking

- a failure to initiate conversation with other children or adults

- 'parroting' or using stereotypical phrases (saying the same expressions over and over again)

- a very restricted vocabulary

- a reluctance to join in group discussions or participate in oral lessons

- difficulty in recalling anything learned by rote (the alphabet, tables, rhymes etc)

- difficulty in recalling information given orally

- a child who gives inappropriate answers during question or discussion times

- a child who only understands literal expressions

- a child who cannot understand jokes

- a child who watches the behaviour of other children in order to know how to act – e.g. does not line up until he/she observes others lining up

- a child who always needs the instructions to be repeated or modified in some way.

Your thoughts

Strategies

There is much that can be done in the classroom to help children with delayed language development, and these strategies will also benefit the class as a whole. Problems associated with delayed development should be largely overcome by the secondary phase. The strategies suggested are equally relevant to children with disordered language. However, such children are also likely to need some support from the speech and language therapy service, so that the nature of their difficulties can be investigated and ways of helping them identified. This is a specialised field, and both school and child should be able to draw on outside expertise. (Speech therapists, who in the past dealt mainly with articulatory problems, now have a much wider role and are able to advise on all aspects of speech and language problems.)

To assist a child with delayed or disordered language development, try some of the following strategies.

- Improve his/her listening skills by keeping information short and straightforward.

- Speak clearly and not too quickly.

- Give the child a good role model.

- Progress the child from listening one-to-one to being able to follow in a small group, then in a class, then as part of the school.

- Don't expect too much of an inattentive child, but work to increase the length of time he or she can concentrate.

- Find out how many commands can be understood and remembered, and work to improve this; for example, if a child can cope with only two commands such as 'Hang up your coat and come and sit down', work towards incorporating a further command – 'Hang up your coat, come and sit down and take out your reading book'.

- Use the child as a messenger, even if at first he or she is only taking a written note.

- Ask questions which need more than a monosyllabic reply.

- When grouping children, ensure that all have a chance to contribute.

- Don't monopolise discussion; it's the children who need the practice!

- Value children's contributions and the place of talk in the classroom.

- Use synonyms to expand vocabulary and to help children put the same information in different ways.

- Encourage the reluctant speaker – he or she may be the one who needs the most practice.

- Encourage children to listen to, and respect, each other's points of view.

- Read aloud, whatever the age of the children – it will improve listening skills and enrich their language.

- Use radio programmes so that children have to concentrate on making use of the auditory channel.

- Expand utterances without appearing to correct them, for example:
  - 'Where you going?'
  - *'Where am I going? I'm going to the staff room. Where are you going?'*
  - 'Go play.'
  - *'You're going out to play, are you?'.*

- Do the same with missing sounds, avoiding over-correction as this can make children self-conscious, for example:
  - 'Bick, peas'
  - *'Do you want a brick?'*
  - 'Bick'
  - *'Here's the brick. May I have another one, please?'.*

- Play memory games.

- Use a tape-recorder (this is useful for the play-back and also as a record of progress).

- Use improvisation, drama, puppets and repetitious songs and stories.

- Give a starting point for discussion – e.g. a television programme, outings, photographs, pictures.

- Make use of rhythm – e.g. tapping or clapping names, phrases, making up question and answer phrases.

- Increase the child's confidence by encouraging relationships with adults and supporting relationships with other children.

- Include the child in small group work as often as resources allow.

- Provide a quiet area in the classroom for talking and listening.

- Modify your language of instruction until you have clear evidence that the child has understood you (without any gestures or contextual support).

- Look for ways to encourage the child to talk more – e.g. using the telephone (a real one, or as a prop).

Autism

Definition

Autism is a developmental disorder which affects social and communication skills and impairs the natural instinct within most people to relate to their fellow human beings. A child with autism shows little curiosity or imagination, frequently seems uninterested or indifferent, and often has an accompanying learning disability. There are approximately four times more males than females with autism.

Autism is considered to be a disability which lies on a continuum, with people being affected to different degrees of severity. **Asperger's Syndrome** is related to autism at the more able end of the spectrum, and children with autism who have been integrated into mainstream provision are often those described as having Asperger's Syndrome.

In some cases, children with autism may have an isolated area of ability – one or two aspects, such as mathematics, art or music, in which they are markedly more advanced than their general developmental level. This is a rare occurrence however, and certainly not typical of children with autism.

It is important to remember that each child with autism is a person in his or her own right with his or her own individual characteristics, as well as those typically displayed by a person with autism.

Identification

Many children with autism will have had their condition identified during their pre-school years, particularly those at the severe end of the continuum. However, children with Asperger's Syndrome may not be identified until they are of statutory school age, when they are sometimes mistaken for children with emotional or behavioural difficulties.

All children with autism will have some impairment in three developmental areas (often referred to as 'the triad of impairments'), although the degree of impairment in each area is individual to each child:

- impairment of social interaction
- impairment of social communication
- impairment of imagination.

The following characteristics are associated with autism, although not all of the following symptoms will necessarily be shown by every autistic child.

- A difficulty understanding or using language.
- Using of limited, repetitious phrases.
- Using of pedantic speech.
- Thinking and talking obsessively about one topic.
- Echoing the speech of others rather than responding appropriately.
- Relying on the situation, rather than words, for meaning.
- Using verbal fluency to disguise a lack of comprehension.
- Interpreting speech in a literal way – e.g. 'it's raining cats and dogs'.
- Using an adult's hand as a 'tool' to indicate what is wanted, rather than communicating needs verbally or pointing.
- Exhibiting bizarre behaviour and mannerisms.

- Making poor use of eye contact.
- Failing to answer when spoken to.
- Being unable to explain actions.
- Making inappropriate social advances.
- Having difficulty with social relationships, and avoiding situations where social interaction is demanded.
- Being unable to empathise with injured or upset children, and displaying indifference to the needs of others.
- Lacking imagination when playing.
- Lacking awareness of common dangers such as deep water or fire.
- Resisting any change in routine, possibly with tantrums.
- Playing with objects in a ritualistic or obsessive way – e.g. spinning or flapping.
- Having an unusual response to sensory stimuli – i.e. sound, light, smell, shadows.
- Preferring activities with mechanical procedures.
- Becoming obsessive or getting 'hooked' on unusual things.

Your thoughts

Strategies

Not all of the following strategies can be put into practice simultaneously, nor are they all appropriate to every individual. As far as possible, maintain good relationships and open lines of communication between school, carers and the family; this will ensure that the child knows what is expected of him/her and is secure in a positive environment.

- Use pictorial instruction and physical prompts to ensure that the child succeeds with new tasks.

- Make eye contact easier for the child by getting down to his or her level when working or playing. Do not turn the child's face up to look at you.

- Give the child longer to do something you have asked before you repeat what you say or give the answer. He or she is likely to need longer to process the instruction.

- Start your instructions with the child's name, as the child with autism often has difficulty in realising that you are addressing your comments and instructions to him/her.

- Actively teach social as well as cognitive and language skills – e.g. teach how to initiate or maintain a conversation by instructing the child where to stand, how to make contact, when to look at the person, what to say, and to wait for the other person to speak.

- Structure learning experiences very carefully.

- Make good use of computers.

- Acknowledge the need for personal space – consider providing an individual work area.

- Teach a whole routine, rather than separate skills to be linked at a later stage – e.g. toilet/wash/dry/coat on.

- Reward action in a natural 'low key' manner.

- Be aware of the child's favourite activity and use it in sequence as the final task and/or instruction (as long as it is not an all-absorbing activity).

- Prepare carefully for new situations, so that children know exactly where they are and what is expected of them.

- Think ahead for the child with autism – talk through, and prepare pictorial clues for a new experience or change of circumstance (a sudden change in timetable for example can cause a traumatic scene). Videos can be very useful for this. Some teachers of children with autism deliberately make changes to the classroom routine and organisation so that the children learn to cope with change.

- Make use of pattern and routine so that the child feels secure.

- Record language samples and analyse them for vocabulary and grammatical structure.

- Revamp stories and rhymes to incorporate new forms of speech patterns, and use new patterns in conversation.

- In the event of a tantrum, distract the child by any acceptable means, or leave and ignore the child if he or she is safe.

- Be aware of the child's current habit or obsession; avoid it if possible, or use it as a reward at an appropriate time.

- Communicate using music: instructions that are sung rather than spoken can be very useful.

- Try 'cloze' procedure with familiar songs – this tempts a non-talker to fill in the gap without realising that he or she has spoken a word.

- Encourage the child to copy rhythms using a variety of instruments.

- Sing and talk using simple rhythms to create a dialogue and effect a response.

- Liaise with all the adults who are involved (carers, specialists and family) in order to ensure that there is consistent management and to focus training and learning programmes.

- Don't rely on verbal directions alone.

- Don't use unclear, non-contextualised gestures as they may confuse the child.

- Don't rely on a child with autism to pick up social knowledge simply by exposure to situations.

- Overwhelm a child with gushing praise or hugs – they may simply alienate him/her.

Useful organisations

AFASIC
2nd Floor
50-52 Great Sutton Street
London EC1V 0DJ
Tel: 020 7490 9410
Helpline: 0845 3555577
Fax: 020 7251 2834
E-mail: info@afasic.org.uk
Web: www.afasic.org.uk

A parent-led organisation to help children and young people with speech and language impairments, and their families.

The Royal College of Speech and Language Therapists
2 White Hart Yard
London SE1 1NX
Tel: 020 7378 1200
Fax: 020 7403 7254
E-mail: postmaster@rcslt.org
Web: www.rcslt.org

Works to improve understanding of all aspects of communication impairment.

I CAN
4 Dyer's Buildings
London EC1N 2QP
Tel: 0870 010 4066
Fax: 0870 010 4067
E-mail: info@ican.org.uk
Web: www.ican.org.uk

A national educational charity for children with speech and language difficulties.

National Autistic Society
393 City Road
London EC1V 1NG
Tel: 020 7833 2299
Helpline: 0870 600 85 85
Fax: 020 7833 9666
E-mail: nas@nas.org.uk
Web: www.nas.org.uk

National Autistic Society Wales
William Knox House
Suite C1, Britannic Way
Llandarcy
Neath SA10 6EL
Tel: 01792 815 915
Fax: 01792 815 911
E-mail: wales@nas.org.uk
Web: www.nas.org.uk

Works to provide education, treatment and care to people with autism and related conditions.

The term **'emotional and behavioural difficulties'** is used in relation to children who have difficulty controlling their behaviour and emotions. Their ability to learn is affected, and they may also find it hard to operate in a social setting. Many children will go through periods when they are anxious, moody or difficult in response to situations that have arisen at home or at school, but the problems of those with emotional and behavioural difficulties are more intractable. Some will become very withdrawn, while others may be disruptive or disaffected. Statistics suggest that boys are more affected by emotional and behavioural difficulties than girls.

Emotional and behavioural difficulties

Children with emotional and behavioural difficulties have sometimes been described as being unlovable and unloved. Indeed, it seems fair to assume that if they become less loveable, it is because they feel unloved. They can make it hard for school staff to build up relationships with them, yet opening positive channels of communication is the main way of reaching them. It takes time and patience to communicate with an uncommunicative child, or to try to understand the disturbed child who, in turn, disturbs the whole class. It is far from easy to strike up a rapport with troubled and troublesome children; even if teachers make the effort, they may not always succeed, but at least they will have given these difficult children a better chance of making a success of their education.

Withdrawn children under-react to situations and may be quiet and passive. They may have a very poor self-image and appear unhappy. They may suffer from depression or a deep-seated feeling of insecurity, or they may be emotionally damaged through physical, sexual or verbal abuse.

By contrast, 'acting-out', aggressive children can be a problem to others as well as themselves. Their inability to fit in to the socially-accepted norms of behaviour make them difficult to control in the classroom. They may have been over-indulged and allowed to believe that their own needs are more important than anyone else's, or they may have become undisciplined through inappropriate social modelling and/or a lack of care, control or understanding.

Recently, the term **'disaffected'** has been used to describe older children who begin to reject their school and its curriculum as irrelevant to their needs.

Identification

The withdrawn child:

- is expressionless, but deeply unhappy

- is over-sensitive to any criticism – unable to tolerate teasing or personal remarks

- has low self-esteem

- is anxious to conform

- lacks interest in work and under-achieves, but may exhibit obsessive behaviour or an all-absorbing interest in a particular hobby or topic

- may be the victim of bullying and try to avoid coming to school

- is a loner, who is ignored by other children rather than being actively disliked

- is unable to form close relationships and is ill at ease in social situations.

It is easy to overlook the withdrawn child whose needs may be just as great as those of the aggressive, disruptive child.

The aggressive child:

- is noisy and demanding, wants his/her own way and immediate attention

- has poor concentration

- is verbally and physically aggressive – will hit out, push, punch and kick, and could be a bully

- shouts out in class and is disruptive

- wanders about and is disobedient

- uses unacceptable language

- disregards rules

- under-achieves

- may truant.

The disaffected child:

- is uninterested in school work

- is unmotivated

- fails to complete homework regularly or on time

- is unimpressed by school rules, particularly those relating to appearance

- lacks consideration for others

- may truant.

Your thoughts

Strategies

Try to find out why the child behaves as he or she does. A greater understanding may help you and your colleagues to empathise rather than perceiving the child as a nuisance. It is important to convey to the child that, while you disapprove of his/her behaviour, you care for him/her as an individual. Try to be consistent in your approach and, where appropriate, work with colleagues to ensure that the same parameters are laid down for the child, whatever the lesson or occasion.

Depending on the nature of the difficulty, some of the following strategies should also help.

- Try to raise the child's esteem by setting tasks where success is achievable, and give the child regular feedback on progress.

- Provide the child with opportunities to take on responsibilities and give praise when these are carried out.

- Find out what kind of reward matters to the child – stars, certificates, praise, choosing an activity etc – and use that approach.

- Liaise closely with parents if at all possible, so that the child knows that the home and the school are working together to help him/her.

- Maintain a positive attitude and encourage the child to do likewise. Make it clear that you expect an improvement, but avoid sarcasm.

- Work on the principle that rewarding appropriate conduct is a more effective way to alter behaviour than punishing inappropriate conduct.

- Establish clear class rules and routines that are understood by all (it may be possible to involve some children with emotional and behavioural difficulties in devising the rules in the first place).

- Try to phrase rules in a positive rather than a negative way.

- Remind children of these rules from time to time, but try to avoid nagging.

- Remember that quiet reprimands can be more effective than a public telling-off.

- Help the child to develop social skills – i.e. knowing how to join in, how to ask for things, how to express his/her point of view.

- Create situations where the child is included in activities first with one other child, and then with a small group. Later on, encourage him/her to join a club or society that he or she will find interesting.

- Find out what his/her interests are, and try to incorporate these in school work, so that motivation increases.

- Be aware of what he or she is good at and provide opportunities for the peer group to recognise these attributes.

- Give as much individual attention and support as possible, so that the child learns that he or she can trust you enough to share his/her worries and concerns.

Other strategies for aggressive children

- Endeavour to become aware of anything that triggers unacceptable behaviour, and intervene or distract the child before the problem occurs.

- Avoid confrontation whenever possible by maintaining eye contact with the child, using his/her name and not becoming emotional. Sound confident and in control, rather than using a loud voice and threatening gestures.

- If a child is too wound up to listen to sense, don't try to reason with him/her but allow a cooling-off period (up to five minutes for younger children, ten to fifteen minutes for older ones).

- When the child has calmed down, try to find time to discuss together what has happened and how it can be avoided the next time.

- Don't expect too much all at once. Work on one aspect of behaviour at a time and reward the child when any progress is made. For example, work on stopping the child calling out for five minutes, then build up to ten minutes and so on. The same strategy is useful to encourage a child to remain seated and 'on task'.

Other strategies for disaffected children

- Give disaffected children an opportunity to talk about their grievances and help them to see the situation from the school's point of view – e.g. why there are rules about dress etc.

- Help disaffected children understand that they will get the most out of school not by rebelling, but by concentrating on the positive aspects: companionship, favourite lessons, clubs and activities etc.

- Encourage children to see that the more they put into school, the more they will get out of it; while they remain negative, school will be an unrewarding experience.

Attention Deficit Disorder (ADD) and Attention Deficit Hyperactivity Disorder (ADHD)

Attention Deficit Disorder (ADD) and Attention Deficit Hyperactivity Disorder (ADHD) affect at least two per cent of the population. These disorders cause children to behave poorly and to under-achieve academically, often despite having a good intellect and good home support. There has been much research into the causes of these conditions in recent years, and it is thought that they are due to an imbalance of chemicals in the brain, especially in the area controlling 'self-monitoring'. Drug therapies such as Ritalin re-balance these chemicals, and in this state of equilibrium the child is able to focus his/her attention. Medication is widely used to treat these conditions and has been shown to be effective in 80 per cent of cases in the short to medium term. Other research looking at the effects of fatty acids in the diet suggests that a change of diet can alter the behaviour of some children.

Children with ADD/ADHD often display:

- a poor concentration span

- difficulty in focusing on conversations or instructions – they do not seem to listen

- difficulty in remembering things, and a propensity to lose things

- a tendency to daydream

- difficulty in organising their work – they cannot prioritise

- problems staying 'on task' and finishing work

- difficulty in staying still

- a need to move quickly – they are always 'on the go'

- a tendency to be restless

- problems with considering the consequences of their actions, and with waiting their turn

- a need for immediate reward

- excessive movements

- over-frequent changes of activity

- co-ordination problems with gross and fine motor skills affected

- problems developing verbal expression – they may have problems sequencing or with stuttering or mumbling

- social clumsiness (misreading social clues, intruding into other people's space).

They are often:
- impulsive

- talkative

- quick tempered

- demanding

- intolerant

- impatient

- unpredictable

- easily frustrated.

Strategies

Children with ADD/ADHD need to be taught how to structure their work, pace activities and manage their emotions.

A structured behaviour programme should:

- build in reminders of what tasks need to be done and by when – tick-lists, diaries, work-plans, etc

- include self-monitoring of completed tasks and behaviour within clearly defined rules

- be consistent

- teach social integration skills

- teach anger management skills.

  It may help if you:

- try to keep instructions, routines and rules short, precise and positive

- make eye contact with the child when speaking

- have very clear routines

- liaise with parents and any other helpful organisations or people

- use a variety of short 'stepped' activities to aid learning

- arrange the room to minimise distractions

- use interesting material.

Tourette's Syndrome

Tourette's Syndrome is one of a number of 'tic' disorders. A 'tic' is an involuntary movement or sound that is repeated over and over again. It is often worse during times of stress or excitement.

Strategies to help an affected child include:

- preventing teasing by making sure other children know and understand the condition

- providing 'time out' when tics become disruptive

- allowing the child to sit at the back of the class so he or she doesn't feel 'stared at'

- have a discreet signal so that the child knows he or she can leave the room to release ticks in private.

Pupil Referral Units (PRUs)

Pupil Referral Units (PRUs) are a type of school established and maintained by an LEA to provide education on a temporary basis for children of compulsory school age who are unable to attend a full-time school.

Children may be referred to PRUs for a wide range of reasons including exclusion from mainstream or special schools, disruptive behaviour, persistent absence from school, medical and psychiatric problems, or special needs which cannot be coped within mainstream or an existing special school and require further assessment. Probably the great majority of children attending them have emotional and behavioural difficulties and most have a background of underachievement. They can be seen as having special educational needs although they may not be statemented or undergoing assessment.

PRUs are intended to offer short-term placements – for younger children at risk of exclusion this may mean dual registration so that they continue on the roll of their school but also attend a PRU where work is undertaken which will support them eventually returning full-time. With older children the emphasis is on preparing them to make a successful transition to further education, training or the world of work. In practice re-integration can be difficult to achieve and some children spend longer than is desirable on roll with a PRU. PRUs offer a range of provision but are most likely to offer part-time placements.

PRUs are not required to teach the national curriculum nor to undertake assessment at the end of key stages. However, with re-integration as an aim, they need to work with reference to the national curriculum although they will be unlikely to be able to offer the full range of subjects.

PRUs may be used inappropriately to cater for children with special educational needs, and it is worrying that successful re-integration from PRUs into mainstream education is often difficult to achieve. However, PRUs can offer a very significant second chance to children who gain in self-esteem and begin to make real progress, both personally and academically.

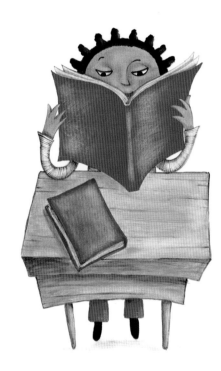

Useful organisations

The Association of Workers for Children with Emotional and Behavioural Difficulties (AWCEBD)
Charlton Court
East Sutton
Maidstone, ME17 3DQ
Tel: 01622 843 104
Fax: 01622 844 220
E-mail: awcebd@mistral.co.uk
Web: www.awcebd.co.uk

Works to promote excellence in services for children who have emotional and behavioural difficulties, and to support those who work with them.

Attention Deficit Disorder Information and Support Service (ADDISS)
PO Box 340
Edgware
Middlesex HA8 9HL
Tel: 030 8906 9068
Fax: 020 8959 0727
E-mail: info@addiss.co.uk
Web: www.addiss.co.uk

Offers advice, information and resources about ADD to parents, young people and professionals.

Tourette's Syndrome (UK) Association
PO Box 26149
Dunfermline KY12 9WT
Tel/Fax: 0845 4 581 252
Web: www.tourettesyndrome.co.uk

Charity dedicated to identifying the cause and controlling the effects of Tourette's Syndrome.

MIND (The Mental Health Charity)
15-19 Broadway
London E15 4BQ
Tel: 020 8519 2122
Info line: 08457 660 163
Fax: 020 8522 1725
E-mail: contact@mind.org.uk
Web: www.mind.org.uk

MIND Cymru
3rd Floor
Quebec House
Castlebridge
5-19 Cowbridge Road East
Cardiff CF11 9AB
Tel: 029 2039 5123
Fax: 029 2040 2041
E-mail: contact@mind.org.uk
Web: www.mind.org.uk

Mental health charity working for those who are diagnosed, labelled or treated as mentally ill. Activities include campaigning, community development, training, publishing and an information service.

GIFTED AND TALENTED CHILDREN

Defining and identifying children as 'gifted' or 'very able' has been fraught with controversy over the years. Taking a normal distribution of pupil attainment, the top 20 per cent are generally now identified as 'able children' and the top two per cent as 'very able'. Under the Government's 'Excellence in Cities' programme, those with evident high attainment or latent high ability in one or more academic subjects are taken to be 'gifted' while those with evident or latent high ability in a creative or an expressive art or in a sport are taken to be 'talented'. These definitions are problematic in themselves, implying that music and art, for example, are in some sense 'not academic'. They also by-pass the vexed issue of 'nature versus nurture.'

Definition

It is widely accepted that able children will have good all-round ability, and will often be divergent thinkers with an aptitude for original ideas. Although learning will come easily to them, they do not necessarily have an easy passage through school. As their intellectual prowess frequently outstrips their social and emotional development, they may find it hard to relate to their peers and to conform. Talented children may also have an uneven pattern of development, since they may have one outstanding talent and yet be otherwise average in attainment.

Apart from spasmodic bursts of concern, very little provision has been made for gifted children, in contrast to the specialist provision that may be available for children with other special educational needs. Few authorities have advisory teachers for very able children and, apart from those who attend one of the handful of specialist schools, they will be found in mainstream classes. Yet the very able child may find it hard to fit in and benefit from the curriculum on offer.

Identification

Children with a particular talent will be readily identified, provided there is scope for them to exercise the talent at school, or if the home/school links are well enough developed for teachers to be aware of this important area of the child's life. Very able children may not necessarily be obvious; some become adept at pretending to be 'average' in order to be accepted, or to avoid being teased. Whereas it is acceptable in a school setting to demonstrate physical prowess, superior intelligence is sometimes mocked by other children. Strangely enough, although our school system is geared to academic success, children who are so able that they feel different do not always thrive. Strenuous efforts should be made to identify gifted and talented children and to meet their needs by stretching them and enabling them to fulfil their potential.

Look out for the child who:

- is exceptionally musical
- excels at sport
- creates three-dimensional working models
- has an advanced moral and social awareness
- is a born leader
- is original, imaginative and creative
- is persistent, resourceful, self-directed and can concentrate for an inordinate amount of time on one topic
- has an unusual hobby, such as astronomy or the study of hieroglyphics
- is inquisitive, sceptical and will argue without giving way
- has an advanced vocabulary
- shows initiative and does not follow the herd
- is versatile and has many interests, although one may be particularly absorbing
- has good judgement and enjoys debating
- has a well-developed sense of humour
- is either unusually extroverted or introverted
- finds it more comfortable and challenging to communicate with adults
- pays great attention to detail
- grasps new concepts with ease
- links areas of knowledge without specific teaching
- is very motivated and self-disciplined
- is a lateral or divergent thinker.

Your thoughts

Strategies

Like other children with special educational needs, very able children need a supportive environment if they are to fulfil their potential. They may have to be helped to become an accepted member of the group. They should be both stretched academically, and praised.

Some of the following strategies may help.

- Make sure the gifted child is not afraid to show his/her ability.

- Recognise the child's individuality, but encourage him/her to mix socially.

- Give stimulating work, so that the child doesn't 'switch off'.

- Provide opportunities for enrichment and working in depth, as opposed to simply accelerating the child's path through the basic curriculum.

- Make sure he or she is sufficiently challenged by giving scope for individual research in an area of interest.

- Encourage the school to build up a resource bank of extension/enrichment material.

- Do not be put off if the child outstrips your knowledge in some areas; treat this as a bonus and make use of it.

- Make use of a research model of working, where both children and teacher operate at the boundaries of their own knowledge.

- Help the child to become self-critical and evaluate his/her own work.

- Give the child responsibility for organising some of his/her own work.

- Help the child to work in a team situation at times.

- Help the child to feel valued as a person, not just because of their unusual gift.

- Try to ensure that he or she has contact with children of similar ability or adults with similar interests.

- Consider whether there is enough flexibility in the system to allow gifted children to work outside their age group for some of the time.

- Provide appropriate, and properly differentiated, homework and school work and ensure that it does not involve irrelevant practice.

- Work closely with parents.

- Encourage the gifted child to take part in games such as chess and bridge.

- Give him/her information about out-of-school clubs and associations involved with able and gifted children.

- Provide information about community resources – for example, museums and theatres.

- Involve parents and encourage them to take the child on visits and answer his/her questions.

Useful organisations

Gifted Children's Information Centre (GCIC)
Hampton Grange
21 Hampton Lane
Solihull B91 2QJ
Tel/Fax: 0121 705 4547

Offers free telephone counselling.

National Association for Gifted Children (NAGC)
Suite 14
14 Challenge House
Sherwood Drive
Bletchley MK3 6DP
Tel: 01908 673 677
Helpline: 0870 770 3217
Fax: 01908 673 679
Web: www.nagcbritain.org.uk

Works to support gifted children and their families. Also provides information regarding gifted children.

The Support Society for Children of High Intelligence
5 Makepeace Avenue
London
N6 6EL
Tel: 020 8347 8927
Web: www.chiorg.ndo.co.uk

A support organisation for the young and intellectually gifted.

Further information and advice for schools about gifted and talented pupils is available from Curriculum Online (www.nc.uk.net/gt/)

SPECIAL EDUCATIONAL NEEDS AND CHILDREN WITH ENGLISH AS AN ADDITIONAL LANGUAGE

6

To quote the 2002 Code of Practice, 'the identification and assessment of the special educational needs of children whose first language is not English requires particular care. Lack of competence in English must not be automatically equated with learning difficulties'.

The United Kingdom is a multicultural and multilingual society, and linguistic diversity is the norm in many classrooms. The term **'bilingual'** can often be an understatement of the number of languages to which a child is exposed and the term **'multilingual'** may actually be a more accurate description of many children.

Definition

The problem with the term **'bilingualism'** is that it gives no indication of the degree of proficiency in the languages spoken.

It is therefore helpful to define the term 'bilingualism' in the following ways.

- **Balanced bilinguals** People who function equally well in two or more languages. Some definitions demand complete fluency in all language skills, including reading and writing. The majority of bilingual children would not fulfil this criterion.

- **Dominant or incipient bilinguals** People who may have only the surface aspects of a second language. The majority of two-language speakers in the United Kingdom fall into this category.

- **Semilinguals** People in whom neither language has been fully developed, preventing them from operating successfully in either language. Although a minority group, there are considerable difficulties involved in dealing with semilingual children.

Bilingual learners may come from any of the following groups:

- those born outside the UK with home languages other than English. This group may include refugees, those with little or no schooling and those with excellent skills in literacy and oracy

- those born in the UK who have little initial experience of English on school entry, as they are not exposed to much English, either at home or in the wider community

- those whose parents have been born and educated in the UK and for whom English is the preferred language for daily communication, although one or more other languages may also be used within the home.

Children from these groups will have different starting points, knowledge about language and experience of using English. There are bilingual children who may have special educational needs in any of the areas identified in the Code of Practice, and these children have the same rights of access to the Code of Practice procedures as monolingual children. Outside agencies who become involved with the child should always be aware of his/her specific requirements with regard to language.

Identification

The Task Group for Assessment and Testing (TGAT) Report of 1988 expected bilingual children to have **'difficulties'** and **'where this problem is so severe'**, exemption from the SATS would be allowed. A **'low level of performance'** is expected, indicating the need for special help in **'English language skills'**.

Clearly, if a child is not a balanced bilingual, he or she will be disadvantaged when being assessed against English Attainment Targets. The subsequent 'low level of performance' may well be regarded as learning difficulty, especially as some of the characteristics of children learning an additional language are similar to characteristics of cognitive difficulties demonstrated by children with special educational needs – e.g. a failure to grasp basic concepts within a subject area, or under-achievement in the area of literacy.

The old assumption made about bilingual children was that they suffered due to having two languages, that in school language should be monolingual and English, and that any under-achievement was due to the mental confusion of having two languages.

The project team for Language in the Curriculum (LINC, 1992) contradicts this view:

> 'This is not so; multilingual language learning is not subtractive… but mutually additive, whereby the growth of competence in one language enhances that in another through constant comparison of the ways the two languages achieve… or sometimes fail to achieve… identical or similar meanings'.

There is also good evidence from cognitive psychology that if both languages are fully maintained, bilingualism is educationally enriching and can have a positive effect on intellectual performance. There will, however, be a minority of children whose progress gives cause for concern. The difficulties of disentangling the differences in

'learning the language' from 'learning difficulties' or special educational needs are compounded when there is an open acknowledgement by educational psychologists that the most traditional assessment procedures are inadequate.

Every person assessing a bilingual child must avoid two potential errors:

- diagnosing a learning difficulty when one is not present, so labelling the child inappropriately, and perhaps instituting an individual education plan (IEP) which may detrimentally alter the method of teaching or place the child into an unsuitable environment

- failing to diagnose a learning difficulty, so not providing entitlement to the Code of Practice processes or specifically targeted and appropriate help.

Your thoughts

Strategies

Consider some of the following strategies to support children.

- Wherever possible, conduct a full bilingual language assessment to determine language proficiency.

- See the first language skills of the children as a valuable potential channel for supporting their learning.

- Do not assume that because a child is fluent in the daily social routines of the classroom (which are often cognitively undemanding and context-embedded), that he or she will be able to perform with a similar level of competency across the curriculum.

- Ensure access to a broad and balanced curriculum: lack of fluency in English need not prevent a bilingual child from working at an appropriately demanding level in mathematics, in arts subjects or in sport.

- Make every effort to ensure that assessment is as culture-fair as possible, even if it cannot be culture-free.

- Use non-verbal tests where possible.

- Carefully review items used in assessment that require verbal or visual recognition, for example:
  - household objects, such as furniture and kitchen utensils
  - vehicle types, such as ambulances and police cars
  - sports equipment or actions
  - outdoor fixtures and building types
  - values represented by pictures such as freedom, honesty, etc
  - professions, such as doctor, judge, fire-fighter
  - clothing
  - historically-related items.

Items such as those above do not need to be omitted but potentially biased items should be marked so that it is possible to monitor how the child performs.

- Remember that straightforward simplification of tasks is not appropriate for bilingual learners – this can result in divorcing the learning from meaning, making the work harder rather than easier to understand.

- Using actual size, real life objects is more successful than trying to operate with abstract concepts.

- Make use of dual language books to allow the parents to support reading development.

- Keep the parents informed. This may mean enlisting the support of an interpreter, but care needs to be exercised as there are issues regarding confidentiality and appropriateness.

Support for children for whom English is an additional language is most fruitfully delivered in the mainstream classroom and any withdrawal should be carefully considered. Within the mainstream classroom, children will still have access to all aspects of the national curriculum, will maintain relationships with their peers and will be exposed to a wider range of language models.

Further reading

A Parents' and Teachers' Guide to Bilingualism
Baker, C (2000)
Multilingual Matters Ltd.
ISBN: 1853 594 563

Helping Refugee Children in Schools
Free leaflet from The Refugee Council
Call 0207 820 3000 for a copy

7 PORTAGE

Portage is a home-visiting educational service for pre-school children who have special needs. It is based on the common-sense principle that parents are the key figures in the care and development of their child. Portage assesses the needs of a child with special education needs, and then, in partnership with parents, builds on the abilities the child already has, teaching skills that the child has yet to master.

A Portage team of home visitors offers a carefully structured but flexible system to help parents become effective teachers of their own children. Portage aims to help parents continue to gain satisfaction and success in their role as the main influence on their child's development. With portage, the parent/child link is consolidated and enriched.

Portage home visitors have wide experience of working with families and children. Among those working as Portage home visitors are teachers, nursery nurses, health visitors, or speech therapists, and everyone involved in providing or managing a service is specially trained in Portage methods.

Increasingly, portage is becoming involved in supporting children with special needs in maintained and private nurseries. The portage service will advise early years settings on ways of including children with a variety of special needs.

Useful organisations

National Portage Association
127 Monks Dale
Yeovil
BA21 3JE
E-mail: npa@portageuk.freeserve.co.uk
Web: www.portage.org.uk

Offers advice and information about portage.

INFORMATION AND COMMUNICATIONS TECHNOLOGY AND SPECIAL EDUCATIONAL NEEDS

8

There are numerous ways in which information and communications technology (ICT) can be used both to support learning and to provide access to learning for children with special educational needs. Its use is most effective when planned as part of a continuing programme. Through the use of ICT resources, children are able to concentrate on the content of learning without being disadvantaged by their particular special needs.

Computers should be used as a tool to aid both the teacher and the child. By using certain software, worksheets can be made more visual with the introduction of pictures or symbols. Word banks can be created to ease the writing process.

It is essential that pupils have access to appropriate ICT resources and that teachers and support staff have appropriate training in specific equipment and software. For some children accessing a computer may be difficult, but there are ways of reducing or solving these problems. In recent years, major developments have taken place in using ICT to provide greater access to all subjects of the curriculum, especially in arts subjects. Subject-specific guidance is issued from time to time by the Qualifications and Curriculum Authority (QCA), the British Educational Communications and Technology Agency (BECTA), and subject associations.

Computer keyboards now come in a variety of sizes. Key guards may be helpful for children with weak muscles who need support for their hands without depressing all the keys. Keyboards can be bought with the letters in alphabetical order as well as in the original 'qwerty' layout.

The computer mouse may be difficult to manipulate for some children. A trackerball may be used as an alternative to a mouse, with the child being able to roll the ball to move the pointer across the screen.

The 'click and drag' operation on the mouse is then converted to a single press on a particular key.

Concept keyboards allow users to design their own overlays and can be used independently or in conjunction with the standard keyboard. Children who tire easily when required to write using the keyboard would find this particularly helpful.

Speech-activated word-processing programmes are now available. These, together with sound and animation, all enhance the use of the technology and act as a motivator for certain users.

LEA support services and other organisations can help assess particular ICT needs for children. For children with statements, some equipment may be funded from the LEA, usually after an assessment of the child's ICT needs has been carried out. Technology is a fast-moving industry and new products are continually being developed. Children's needs also change, and so it will often be necessary for ICT assessment to take place on a regular basis.

Useful organisations

Aiding Communication in Education (ACE)
Centre Advisory Trust
92 Windmill Road
Oxford OX3 7DR
Tel: 01865 759 800
Fax: 01865 759 810
E-mail: info@ace-centre.org.uk
Web: www.ace-centre.org.uk

Aiding Communication in Education (ACE) – North
Broadbent Road
Watersheddings
Oldham OL1 4HU
Tel: 0161 627 1358
Fax: 0161 627 0363
E-mail: enquiries@ace-north.org.uk
Web: www.ace-north.org.uk

An independent charity offering information, support
and training for parents and professionals in the use
of technology for young people who have
communication difficulties.

Advisory Unit: Computers in Education
126 Great North Road
Hatfield AL9 5JZ
Tel: 01707 266714
Fax: 01707 273684
E-mail: sales@advisory-unit.org.uk
Web: www.advisory-unit.org.uk

Independent organisation offering IT services and
educational software to schools – can offer specific
information on special needs requirements.

Inclusive Technology Ltd
Gateshead Business Park
Delph New Road
Oldham OL3 5BX
Tel: 01457 819 790
Fax: 01457 819 799
E-mail: inclusive@inclusive.co.uk
Wob: www.inclusive.co.uk

Suppliers of a range of resources that facilitate the
use of technology by people with special needs.

British Educational Communications and Technology Agency (BECTA)
Milburn Hill Road
Science Park
Coventry CV4 7JJ
Tel: 024 7641 6994
Fax: 024 7641 1418
E-mail: becta@becta.org.uk
Web: www.becta.org.uk/inclusion/

The Government's lead agency on the use of ICT in
education. Produces a wide range of factsheets
on using ICT in special needs and inclusive education.

SEMERC – Granada Learning
Quay Street
Manchester M60 9EA
Tel: 0161 827 2719
Fax: 0161 827 2966
E-mail: sis@granadamedia.com
Web: www.granada-learning.com/special_needs

The special needs division of Granada Learning – offers
advice to teachers and parents on ICT, curriculum and
special needs issues.

FURTHER EDUCATION AND SPECIAL EDUCATIONAL NEEDS

9

Much of the practical information on SEN in this booklet will be relevant to students and lecturers in further education (FE), although clearly structures and access to services are not the same as in the maintained school sector.

It is not a statutory requirement for an FE college to have a special educational needs co-ordinator or someone with a similar title to oversee special educational needs provision, but Government guidelines recommend it and most colleges will have one. The same is true of staff to support students with special educational needs in mainstream teaching sessions. Although these are not statutory, FE colleges must 'have regard to' the special educational needs of students, and in some instances this will mean providing support staff in mainstream teaching. If the college has a special unit, for example for teaching independent living skills to students with learning difficulties, its staff may well be involved in supporting these students (often unobtrusively) when they mix with other students in social situations or activities.

Funding for additional learning support in FE is provided by the Learning and Skills Council, which has a specific statutory duty to consider the needs of people with learning difficulties and/or disabilities in discharging its duties. Providers funded by the Council must have regard to the Disability Discrimination Act 1995 and the Special Educational Needs and Disability Act 2001. A distinction is made between additional **learning support** (teaching etc.) and **learner support** (equipment, special transport, signers for the deaf, costs of childcare etc.).

Additional learning needs are assessed using diagnostic tools or a statement of special educational need. Information to inform assessment should be passed on by the Connexions service.

A separate category of **additional social needs** is also recognised, and these are identified via a list of nine 'barriers to employment'.

To support a disabled student within mainstream further or higher education, the university or college needs to enable the student to access not only direct teaching – lectures, tutorials and seminars – but also libraries, information and materials relevant to the course, facilities within the college, practical activities, general welfare services and, if necessary, accommodation. There are also social life needs, in particular interaction and socialising with fellow students. For students with a sensory impairment, a college-wide policy on communication is necessary to enable integration and inclusion of students with their peers. Specific awareness training is therefore essential.

Support should be forthcoming from the college staff and through the college's disability officer and Students' Union. Consulting with the student to identify his/her needs will help colleges to address them and to put in place relevant provision. The most important need to be established is communication and the method by which the student can best access teaching.

For students with a sensory impairment, these needs are generally addressed by using the most relevant interpreting method:
- British Sign Language (BSL)
- hands on signing
- deafblind manual alphabet
- keyboard interpreting, with dialogue interpreted through either large print or Braille
- Sign Sighted English (SSE)
- Tadoma
- lipspeaking.

The structure of lectures, tutorials and seminars should be reconsidered in order to address practical implications arising from the use of interpreters.

The following issues should also be considered:
- the environment
- interpreter-breaks
- an awareness on the part of fellow students and tutors.

Mainstream provision is not appropriate for all SEN students. For example, the nature of deafblindness in particular often results in developmental delay. There is specialist college provision for deafblind young people, based on the belief that this group have the right to a continuing education programme, and that they have much still to achieve between the ages of 19 and 24. The focus of this further education centres on developing independence, social and life skills within a supported communicating environment. Frequently, residential colleges enable a 24-hour learning programme and consistent communication support in a variety of settings.

For advice about students with special needs, lecturers' first point of reference should be the SENCo or their equivalent at the college. Most FE colleges (except very small institutions) will also have a college nurse who can give some advice on medical aspects of special educational needs. Since FE colleges have become incorporated and independent of local education authorities (except in Northern Ireland), they are no longer entitled to look to LEA advisers for specialist help and support, although formal or informal arrangements with LEAs may exist in some areas.

The main external sources of support and advice on special needs for FE colleges will be local Learning and Skills Councils (in England) or the Further Education Funding Council for Wales. Informal networks of lecturers working in special educational needs also exist, and the Learning and Skills Development Agency run courses for the professional development of further education staff.

Useful organisations

Skill: National Bureau for Students with Disabilities
Chapter House
18-20 Crucifix Lane
London SE1 3JW
Tel: 020 7450 0620
Information Service line: 0800 328 5050
Fax: 0207450 0650
E-mail: info@skill.org.uk
Web: www.skill.org.uk

Skill in Northern Ireland
Unit 2
Jennymount Court
North Derby Street
Belfast BT15 3HN
Tel: 01232 287 000
Fax: 01232 287 007
E-mail: admin@skillni.demon.co.uk

Promotes opportunities for young people and adults with any kind of disability in post–16 education, training and employment. Provides individual support and advice as well as a range of printed material. Publisher of 'A guide to the Disability Discrimination Act' (£12.50, 2000), which offers an account of the law for further and higher education institutions.

Consortium of Higher Education Support Services for Deaf Students (CHESS)
Access and Guidance
Sheffield Hallam University
Howard Street
Sheffield S1 1WB

A support network of people in higher education supporting deaf students.

The Learning and Skills Council
Cheylesmore House
Quinton Road
Coventry CV1 2WT
Tel: 0845 019 4170
Fax: 024 7649 3600
E-mail: info@lsc.gov.uk
Web: www.lsc.gov.uk

Responsible for funding and planning education and training for over 16-years-olds in England.

Learning and Skills Development Agency
Regent Arcade House
19-25 Argyll Street
London W1F 7LS
Tel: 020 7297 9000
Fax: 020 7297 9001
E-mail: enquiries@lsda.org.uk
Web: www.lsda.org.uk

Strategic national resource for the development of policy and practice in post-16 education and training.

Dysg (Welsh operation of the LSDA)
Quadrant Centre
Cardiff Business Park
Llanishen
Cardiff CF14 5WF

Supports the development of policy and assists in its implementation across all post-16 education and training in Wales.

Further Education Funding Council for Wales
Linden Court
The Orchards
Ilex Close
Cardiff CF14 5DZ
Tel: 029 2076 1861
Fax: 029 2076 3163
E-mail: feinfo@wfc.ac.uk
Web: www.wfc.ac.uk

Responsible for further education funding in Wales.

APPENDIX 1
The role of Special Educational Needs Coordinators (SENCos)

The revised SEN Code of Practice (2002) outlines the roles and responsibilities of the SENCo as follows:

'the SENCo… working closely with the headteacher, senior management and fellow teachers, should be closely involved in the strategic development of the SEN policy and provision. The SENCo has responsibility for day-to-day operation of the school's SEN policy and for co-ordinating provision for children with SEN, particularly through School Action and School Action Plus.' (paragraph1:39)

It also states that the key responsibilities of the SENCo may include:

- overseeing the day-to-day operation of the school's SEN policy

- co-ordinating provision for children with special educational needs

- liaising with and advising fellow teachers

- managing learning support assistants

- overseeing the records of all children with special educational needs

- liaising with parents of children with special educational needs

- contributing to the in-service training of staff

- liaising with external agencies including the LEAs' support and educational psychology services, health and social services, and voluntary bodies.
(Paragraphs 5.32 and 6.35)

The revised SEN Code of Practice states quite unequivocally that SENCo's need adequate non-contact time for planning and co-ordination, record-keeping, managing and supporting learning support assistants, observing children, and liaising with colleagues and other schools. (See paragraphs 5.33 and 6.36.)

It also states that it would be inappropriate for a SENCo to have other management responsibilities, the role being 'at least equivalent to that of curriculum, literacy or numeracy co-ordinator', (see paragraphs 5.34 and 6.37.) and implies that it will usually be appropriate for the SENCo to be a member of the leadership group.

SENCos should also have access to ICT for SEN management systems and for preparing and recording IEPs. They should also be able to communicate with other SENCos through the SENCo Forum, co-ordinated by the British Educational Communications and Technology Agency (BECTA), at **www.becta.org.uk/inclusion/discussion/** (Paragraphs 5.36 and 6.39)

SENCos can only fulfil their responsibilities if they have the full support of governors, senior management and their colleagues, and of the LEA.

Recommendations for SENCos:
- get training on time management – you will need it
- pace yourself
- admit you don't know things – ask for expert help
- request staff support – special educational needs is everyone's responsibility, not just the SENCo's
- maintain close dialogue with your headteacher and with the SEN governor.

APPENDIX 2
Useful organisations

The Alliance for Inclusive Education
Unit 2
70 South Lambeth Road
London SW8 1RL
Tel: 020 7735 5277
Fax: 020 7735 3828
E-mail: info@allfie.org
Web: www.allfie.org.uk

A national network offering materials and ideas for people interested in inclusive education.

Association of Educational Psychologists
26 The Avenue
Durham DH1 4ED
Tel: 0191 384 9512
Fax: 0191 386 5287
Web: www.aep.org.uk

Professional association and trade union for education psychologists in England, Wales and Northern Ireland.

British Psychological Society
St Andrews House
48 Princess Road East
Leicester LE1 7DR
Tel: 0116 254 9568
Fax: 0116 247 0787
E-mail: enquiry@bps.org.uk
Web: www.bps.org.uk

Responsible for the development and promotion of psychology, and for the application of psychology for the public good.

Centre for Studies on Inclusive Education (CSIE)
Room 2S 203 S Block
Frenchay Campus
Coldharbour Lane
Bristol BS16 1QU
Tel: 0117 344 4007
Fax: 0117 344 4005
Web: http://inclusion.uwe.ac.uk

Offers information and advice about inclusive education and related issues.

Department for Education and Skills
Sanctuary Buildings
Great Smith Street
London SW1P 3BT
Tel: 08700 012345
Web: www.dfes.gov.uk/sen/

Government department responsible for education. The 'SEN' section of the website provides a wide range of advice and materials for teachers, parents and others interested in or working with children with special educational needs.

Disability Wales
Wernddu Court
Caerphilly Business Park
Van Road
Caerphilly CF83 3ED
Tel: 029 2088 7325
Fax: 029 2088 8702
E-mail: info@dwac.demon.co.uk
Web: www.dwac.demon.co.uk

National association of disability groups in Wales

Independent Panel for Special Education Advice (IPSEA)
6 Carlow Mews
Woodbridge
Suffolk IP12 1EA
Tel: 01394 380 518
Advice line for England and Wales: 0800 018 4016
Advice line Northern Ireland: 01232 705 654
Web: www.ipsea.org.uk

Offers free independent advice on special educational needs, advice on appealing to the Special Educational Needs Tribunal, and second professional opinions.

National Association for Special Educational Needs
NASEN House
4/5 Amber Business Village
Amber Close
Amington
Tamworth B77 4RP
Tel: 01827 311 500
Fax: 01827 313 005
E-mail: welcome@nasen.org.uk
Web: www.nasen.org.uk

Aims to promote the education, training, advancement and development of all those with special educational needs. Has over sixty branches across the country and 11,500 members.

National Children's Bureau (NCB)
8 Wakley Street
London EC1V 7QE
Tel: 020 7843 6000
Fax: 020 7278 9512
E-mail: library@ncb.org.uk
Web: www.ncb.org.uk

The centre of several networks through which professionals involved in supporting children can learn from each other and develop policy.

Special Educational Needs Joint Initiative for Training
Institute of Education
University of London
20 Bedford Way
London WC1H 0AL
Tel: 020 7612 6000
Fax: 020 7612 6126
E-mail: info@ioe.ac.uk
Web: www.ioe.ac.uk

A partnership between the Institute of Education and local authorities which provides short courses, support groups, local training and consultancy for teachers and other professionals working with children with special educational needs.

APPENDIX 3
The Association of Teachers and Lecturers Special Educational Needs Advisory Committee 2001/2002

Angie Rutter (Chair)
Ian Griffiths (Vice Chair)
Sandy Cooke (Secretary)
Pat Preihs
Glynne Rowlands

Sharon Camilletti
Graham Evans
Angela Forkin
Pat Griffiths
Ian Morrison
Karen Rogers

YOUR NOTES:

The Association of Teachers and Lecturers exists to promote the cause of education generally in the
UK and elsewhere, to protect and improve the status of teachers, lecturers, and other non-teaching professionals
directly involved in the delivery of education, and to further the legitimate and professional interests of all our members.

For a free copy of the Association of Teachers and Lecturers' publications catalogue, please call 0845 4500 009.

First published 1998, revised 2002.

To receive the text of this book in large font, please contact ATL.